D0517624

Your *Baby,*
Your Body

Your *Baby,* Your Body

Fitness During Pregnancy

Carol Stahmann Dilfer

CROWN PUBLISHERS, INC., NEW YORK

©1977 by Carol Stahmann Dilfer

All rights reserved. No part of this book may be reproduced or utilized
in any form or by any means, electronic or mechanical, including
photocopying, recording, or by any information storage and retrieval
system, without permission in writing from the publisher.
Inquiries should be addressed to Crown Publishers, Inc.,
One Park Avenue, New York, New York 10016

Printed in the United States of America

Published simultaneously in Canada by
General Publishing Company Limited

Book Design: Huguette Franco

Library of Congress Cataloging in Publication Data
Dilfer, Carol Stahmann.
    Your baby, your body: Fitness during pregnancy.

    Bibliography: p.
    Includes index.
    1. Prenatal care. 2. Exercise for women. I. Title.
[DNLM: 1. Pregnancy—Popular works. 2. Gymnastics. WQ150 D576y]
RG525.D54 1977   618.2'4   77-5883
ISBN 0-517-52855-X (cloth)
ISBN 0-517-528658 (paper)

10 9 8 7 6 5

Dedication

This book is for my parents, Ben and Bette Stahmann

*I*t wouldn't be fair to say that I wrote this book by myself. Throughout the process of its completion I received a great deal of support and encouragement from many friends. My sincere thanks to Andrea Danzig, who believed this book would happen even before I did; to Robbie Fanning, a friend, fellow writer, and jogging companion, for her constant support and helpful suggestions; to my agent, Elyse Sommer, for handling the logistics with such goodwill; to my husband, Bob, for supporting my "creative spirit"; to all the women who have participated in my class, and from whom I have learned so much; to my models, Jan Mangione, Lynne Morrall, Jill Phillips, Susie Richardson, and Carol Whiteley, for giving so freely of their time and loving energy; and to my children, Michael and Heather, for respecting my grumpy hat, and for believing that their mom is a writer.

Contents

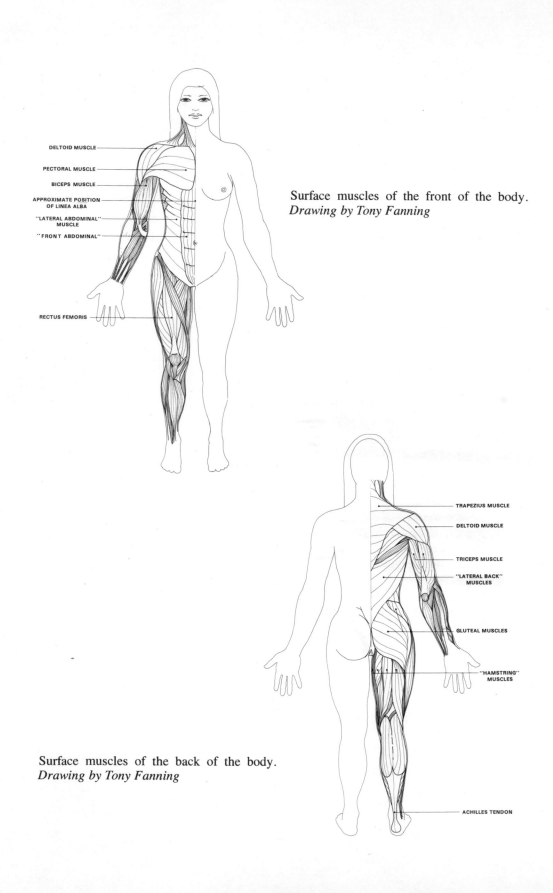

DELTOID MUSCLE

PECTORAL MUSCLE

BICEPS MUSCLE

APPROXIMATE POSITION
OF LINEA ALBA

"LATERAL ABDOMINAL"
MUSCLE

"FRONT ABDOMINAL"

RECTUS FEMORIS

Surface muscles of the front of the body.
Drawing by Tony Fanning

TRAPEZIUS MUSCLE

DELTOID MUSCLE

TRICEPS MUSCLE

"LATERAL BACK"
MUSCLES

GLUTEAL MUSCLES

"HAMSTRING"
MUSCLES

ACHILLES TENDON

Surface muscles of the back of the body.
Drawing by Tony Fanning

Pregnant Does Not Equal Fat

*N*o, you *don't* have to get fat during pregnancy, or afterwards either, for that matter. Not even if your mother did, and your grandmother, and all your sisters, and three of your four first cousins. It doesn't have to happen to *you*. You're different. Your body is your body—not your mother's body or your grandmother's body. And by working with your body you can avoid becoming one of tomorrow's dumpy young mothers.

How? Watch what you eat. And *exercise!* Now, I'm not saying that it's *easy* to exercise. It isn't always. It means creating time, and making yourself a firm promise (a *firm* promise; a girl-scout's-honor promise) to spend 120 minutes a week exercising. And that time must be sacred! Don't let anyone take it away from you. And for heaven's sake, don't do the dishes then. Ironically, you may find that the dishes are your strongest temptation to stray. Or the dusting. Or the vacuuming. Or last week's laundry. But don't let that housekeeping urge trap you. It's just another excuse (there are plenty of others) not to exercise. The dishes will still be there later. And so will all the other chores. Housework is like a hydra—chop off one head and thirteen more spring up. Ignore them—just for 120 minutes—and do something nice for *you*. You have to live in that body of yours for the rest of your life. Take care of it now and it won't betray you later by aching or sagging into pooches and rolls where there weren't any.

You're probably wondering if it's safe to exercise during pregnancy. Yes. Yes!

YES! Provided, of course, that you approach it sensibly and regularly, and that the exercises you do are based on a firm understanding of the physiology of pregnancy. And the ones I'm including are.

I don't guarantee that this book will solve all your problems of self-image or weight control or lack of self-discipline. But I'll tell you what I *will* do in this book. I'll explain—in part—how your body is different now from what it was when you were not pregnant, and tell you how to take that knowledge into consideration when planning your exercise program. I'll talk to you about the need for proper posture and why sloppy posture undermines even the *best* exercise program. I'll give you a twenty-minute regular calisthenic routine that, done regularly, will make (and keep) your body firm and limber. And I'll also provide additional exercises to substitute for those you loathe in the regular routine, or for extra work on those parts of your body that you want to look even more smashing *after* you deliver your baby than they did *before* you became pregnant. And I'll give you instructions on how to create your own exercise program if you hate the one I've provided. I really do believe that, in the end, the only exercise program you'll really stick to is one that suits your own personality and way of life. There's no reason on earth to look at the one I'm providing as gospel. It's only for starts. If you hate it, create your own. I'll tell you how. I'll talk to you about aerobic exercises, why they are important, and how to work them into your schedule. I'll teach you how to relieve—at least temporarily—some of those aches and pains that so many pregnant women experience. And, finally, I'll provide you with a list of recommended reading on other aspects of pregnancy and mothering, as well as a list of national organizations dedicated to the health, education, and welfare of pregnant women and their mates.

Now a couple of words about what this book will *not* do for you. I won't try to bluff you into thinking that exercise is the greatest thing since hot fudge sundaes. Truth is that exercise, especially if you are really out of shape and unused to using your body, takes discipline and a no-nonsense kind of dedication. There's no way that I'll try to convince you that by doing these exercises your labor will be one of those sixty-minute wonders that *everybody's* neighbor seems to have had. Labor is *hard* work. But a body that is flexible and strong works much more efficiently and tires less easily as a result of the work than does a body that has been neglected. (It looks better too.) That's true anytime in life. And it's true during pregnancy and labor. I won't try to persuade you that by doing twenty-five roll-ups and a few thigh firmers you will shed that old cocoon and emerge as a sylphlike butterfly. I won't pretend that you can get away with eating twice as much now that you are exercising. (That would be an out and out *lie*.) And I won't kid you into thinking that jogging around the block guarantees happiness.

What you *will* find, after you've been exercising a few weeks, is that you sleep better and need less time in the sack; that you lose inches even if you don't lose weight; that your back (or neck or head) doesn't ache quite so often or quite so badly; that work doesn't fatigue you as much; that movement—all kinds of movement—feels better; that you will probably begin to experience your body in a new, more positive way; and that, as you stand in front of the mirror and look at that belly bulge, you will feel positively, deliciously smug, for you will be fighting back.

Practically nothing in life is guaranteed. But under normal circumstances, if you work regularly with your body, you'll get results—*good* results. Your muscles will become stronger and more elastic; you will become more flexible and less achy; your whole body will become firmer and trimmer. You will feel better—all over. That's the truth.

1

Of Course You Can Exercise During Pregnancy

*H*ow many times have you heard that pregnant women should take it easy—relax, read a lot, sit down most of the day. Or that pregnant women should not bend over (that might squash the baby). Or not stretch their arms above their heads (never can tell when the baby might strangle on its own umbilical cord). Or, for heaven's sake, never do such strenuous things as take walks or ride a bike or play tennis. Plenty of times? Me too. But to all of that I say . . . HORSEFEATHERS!

It simply is not true that a pregnant woman should not exercise. Bodies *need* to work throughout life if they are to remain strong and healthy, and pregnancy is no exception. But those fairy tales are scary. And we've all heard them so often that we half believe them in spite of our rational selves.

At least *I* did when I was pregnant with my first child, Michael. I believed them so much that I even quit dancing—which had been my fitness program, my creative outlet, my therapy all rolled into one. It almost killed me. But a gnarled old woman had once looked me straight in the eye and warned me, with complete sincerity too, that if I kept dancing I would surely have a miscarriage. And then, my doctor (who should have known better—I was, after all, healthy and experiencing a normal pregnancy) advised me to be very, very careful. That did it. I bought the whole shebang.

But by the time I was pregnant for the third time I had learned better. During that pregnancy, I not only danced, but I jogged a couple of miles four times a week, and led fitness classes as well. And do you know what? Not only was my beautiful daughter, Heather, a full-term, healthy baby, but I felt *great* during that pregnancy—no backaches, no throbbing legs. My delivery was long, but easy; my recovery rapid. And I looked great after I delivered Heather too.

So if your pregnancy is normal and uncomplicated, it is fair to be suspicious of all those dire prophesies about the terrible effects of moderate exercise upon pregnancy. I speak from lots of experience with pregnant women and exercise. To date, over four hundred women have participated in my prenatal fitness classes. They have come in all states of fitness and unfitness, and I know of no complications resulting from exercise—not even one. *And* I know of lots of good things that have resulted from the exercise. These four hundred women speak strongly to me; I trust their experiences, and I think that you can too.

Still, folklore *does* abound, especially about exercise inducing miscarriage. It's hogwash, of course, but it's *pervasive* hogwash. The truth is that, given a pregnancy with no maternal problems, a fetus is aborted only when it is dead.

A healthy fetus is as safe in your body as is a goldfish in a tightly sealed, water-filled sack. Turn the sack upside down, shake it, drop it, and the fish is just fine. The water protects it from harm. It is the same with your baby.

But why would you *want* to exercise during pregnancy?

I can think of several reasons. Perhaps you would like to keep your weight gain to a respectable twenty-four pounds. Maybe your back aches or your legs throb, and you're tired of putting up with the discomfort and inconvenience. Maybe you are afraid of a postpartum potbelly. Maybe you would like to swim once in a while and not be exhausted by the effort. Perhaps you'd enjoy feeling really alive after 6:30 P.M. Or maybe you'd like to sleep a little better at night. Perhaps you'd like to take Susi to the park and play with her instead of just sitting—heavily—on the bench. Maybe you fear that if a flight of stairs leaves you exhausted, you'll never be able to cope with the demands of a newborn. Maybe you have finally lost the battle with tightly closed pickle jars. Maybe you would like to feel better in general—less tired, more able to enjoy things—to have more energy so that you can exert yourself a bit and not need to sleep most of the day afterward. Maybe daily tension is spoiling your fun and you'd rather dispel it through exercise than by hitting the bottle. Or perhaps you would just like to experience the joy and sense of control that comes from using your body the way it is meant to be used.

These are all good reasons to begin a fitness program. Anytime in life. During pregnancy too.

Of course, there is the obvious reason as well: You are going to have a baby. Now, it is not necessary to be physically fit to deliver that baby. Under normal circumstances, your baby *will* be born; somehow that takes care of itself.

So why bother with exercise? Because, as artists say, the truth of the materials will be known. In this case, the material is your body. And truth has something to do with strength and stamina, how efficiently you labor and deliver, and how quickly you recover afterward.

A weak, flabby, deconditioned body can deliver a baby—no doubt about it. But it pays for it later—aching shoulders, tight inner thighs, sore perineal area, fatigue. Oh! the fatigue!

A strong conditioned body, on the other hand, fares much better. It may labor as long as the flabby body, but it will work much more easily and efficiently. And it will not be nearly as fatigued by the work.

Doctors have repeatedly told me two things about exercise during pregnancy. First, that strong abdominal and pelvic floor muscles make for an easier delivery (especially during transition and pushing). And, second, that women with strong hearts and respiratory muscles, with efficient circulation, and good oxygen delivery not only labor more easily and efficiently, but they recover much faster.

So there you are. Fitness not only can improve your appearance and the quality of your life. Fitness can also make your labor, delivery, and postpartum recovery much easier.

Now comes the crunch. Fitness does not just happen. You must *make* it happen.

If you are an active person by nature, you are probably fit already. The exercise program in this book can help you maintain that fitness, strengthen areas that you may normally neglect, and contribute to increased flexibility. But basically this is just icing on an already fine cake.

If, however, you are by nature or situation inactive, then chances are that you are unfit. In that case, you need this book to help you achieve and maintain physical fitness.

To be truly fit you must develop and maintain a strong, flexible musculo-skeletal system, a trained cardiovascular system, and enough stamina and reserve to cope with the stresses of daily life (and, when necessary, additional stress). What this means is: Your muscles must have both strength (the ability to perform work); and endurance (the ability to work for a long time without undue fatigue); your heart should be strong enough to cope with about an hour's worth of moderate exercise; your respiratory muscles must be strong and flexible enough to allow full expansion of your lungs; your blood vessels must have good tone and must efficiently deliver blood (and the oxygen and other nutrients it contains) to *all* parts of your body. Once you have achieved this, you will have stamina and endurance as well.

Still, within that definition of fitness, there are many levels of adequate fitness, and the first thing you should do is decide just how fit you want to become. If you want to run a marathon a year from now, you'll need more assistance than this book can offer. But if your goals are to have better muscle tone, more energy, greater reserve and stamina, more flexibility; to look and feel better, both during your pregnancy and afterward, then this book is for you.

Done regularly—I repeat, done *regularly*—the aerobic and calisthenic exercises provided here will allow you to attain all these goals. But always remember, the first rule of fitness is to exercise regularly, because sporadic exercise not only does little good, but is potentially more harmful than no exercise at all. If you forget a day, or are sick and need to stop for a while, or are on vacation and find exercising inconvenient, don't worry. That happens to everyone sometimes. The important thing is not to let a temporary layoff become a permanent one. Begin your regular exercise program again as soon as possible.

The second rule of fitness can be stated in three words: easy does it. Your exercise sessions should be relaxing and enjoyable. You should never strain. You should never feel pain. You don't need to sweat like crazy. You don't have to ache afterward. If, at any time, the exercise seems more like sheer drudgery than fun (fun is relative, remember), it is time to rethink. Perhaps your setting is not right. Try putting on some music while you exercise. Or farming the children out to friends. Or watching a favorite television show. Or finding other pregnant women to keep you company. (If all else fails and your obstetrician can't provide companions, run a press release in your local paper.) Perhaps you are expecting too much of yourself and pushing too hard. You should know that you cannot become totally fit in two weeks no matter *how* hard you work. And working too hard will probably only lead to aches, pains, fatigue, even injury. So relax a little (relax a *lot*). Work within *your* body's limits, and expand those limits only a little at a time. Fitness *will* come if you exercise regularly; give it time.

Fitness does not have to be the result of the spartan endeavor that so often characterizes exercise classes—it can (and I think *should)* be achieved gently. But to become fit it *is* necessary to work a little harder than usual. This is the principle of overload. Your body will adapt to the demands put upon it. It becomes as fit as it must to meet your physical activity requirements. So overload happens when you do six roll-ups when you normally do only five, or when the five roll-ups you do are of a more difficult nature than your old version. Or when you jog for twenty minutes instead of the usual fifteen. The tiniest bit of extra effort will contribute to increased fitness. And each tiny step, taken when your body is ready for it, will make it that much easier to take the next step.

Remember, too, that in the matter of fitness your body is much wiser than your mind. It will tell you when it needs more. Or when it has had enough. Listen to it!

2

Some of the Ways Your Body Changes During Pregnancy

*J*ust in case nobody has told you, pregnancy is such an amazing physio-logical phenomenon that practically nothing in your body is the same now as it was before you became pregnant.

That's pretty astonishing when you think about it. Not only is your belly becoming larger, but your blood volume is increased, your heart function is different, as is your hormonal balance. Even your skin and your fingernails and your hair are different. So are your joints. Now, clearly, with all these changes (and more! more!) going on, it would be pretty impossible—not to mention presumptuous—to talk about all of them here.

But if you are going to exercise, you should know about *some* of these bodily changes.

INCREASED WEIGHT AND BULK

It is obvious that pregnancy results in increased weight and bulk, especially during the last trimester (last three months).

Most women can expect to gain a minimum of twenty-four pounds by the end of their pregnancies. The weight gain is divided about like this:

Infant . . . . .7 pounds
Placenta . . . . .1 pound
Amniotic Fluid . . . . .1½ pounds
Uterus . . . . .2½ pounds
Breasts . . . . .3 pounds
Protein and Fluid Stored by Mother . . . . .8½ pounds

As you become larger and heavier, you will probably find that your increased size causes some inconvenience. For example, it is more difficult to move when you are heavier. And there is no getting around the fact that it is harder to bend over, get up, etc. with a big belly than it is with a flat one. You may find that balance becomes a problem. And for sure you will find that, by the end of your pregnancy, some of the exercises in this book will be more difficult than they were previously.

The exercises that you'll probably have most difficulty with are those that involve bending forward from your hips (toe touches, roll-ups, etc.). As your baby takes up more room between your pelvic bones and your rib cage, it becomes harder

5

and harder to remain flexible between those two points. You will also probably need to slow down the pace of the aerobics part of your exercise program. There is simply more of you to move around late in pregnancy, and that takes more energy.

So be it. But, despite all that, keep exercising anyway. As long as you're *trying,* you will benefit from the exercises.

You can do all the exercises recommended in this book—unless your doctor tells you specifically not to—until you deliver your baby. And then, once you feel up to it, you can begin them again after your baby is born. (It is best to wait at least a week after delivery to begin any form of sit-up, though; let your uterus find its place again.)

RELAXIN

Beginning early in pregnancy, your body secretes a hormone called Relaxin. Its job, as far as we know, is to "relax" pelvic joint tissue (the stuff that holds bone to bone and bone to muscle) in preparation for delivery.

But Relaxin, being nondiscriminatory, affects not only pelvic joint tissue, but connective tissue throughout your body. That means that *all* your joints, as well as your spine, are a little bit looser, and perhaps a little bit weaker now than when you are not pregnant.

In order to protect your joints and spine, it is very important to warm up your joints before each exercise session. (I've provided joint warm-ups. See #s 1–5.) Warm-ups prepare your joints and related tissue for more strenuous exercise in two ways. They cause the synovial membranes in your joints to secrete synovial fluid, a lubricant that allows the bones to move more easily. And they cause the joint collagen tissue to become shorter and thicker, and therefore stronger.

It is also important to wear good shoes if you plan to jog during pregnancy. Make certain that your jogging shoes have good arch supports and good cushioning in the soles. I recommend wearing jogging shoes made for hard surface running. But try not to run on hard surfaces such as concrete and asphalt; run on grass or a track instead. This will make jogging considerably less stressful on your joints.

BREAST CHANGES

If you looked at how weight gain is distributed by the end of pregnancy, you noticed that there is an average weight gain of three pounds in the breasts alone.

Breasts are glands that contain no muscle tissue. And so it is impossible to firm up breast tissue by exercise, although you *can* firm up the pectoral muscles that lie *underneath* the breasts. Most women find that their breasts are not as firm and well shaped after they have had a baby as they were before they became pregnant. So I think that it's only fair to tell you that you may experience the same thing. But you can minimize the amount of change if you wear a good supportive bra (without elastic straps) during your pregnancy, and especially during exercise. If you are big breasted naturally, it is even more important to wear a bra during exercise, not only because it will help prevent droopy postpartum breasts, but because it will be more comfortable.

ROUND LIGAMENTS

Round ligaments attach to the top of each side of your uterus and run diagonally from there to your pelvic floor. Their job is to keep your uterus in midline.

When you are not pregnant your uterus is a solid organ weighing about one ounce. By the end of pregnancy it has become a thin-walled sac weighing about two and one-half pounds.

Clearly, your uterus expands a great deal during pregnancy, and as it expands round ligaments must stretch. But, round ligaments, like all ligamental tissue, are not very elastic. And sometimes if they are stretched too suddenly, you may feel short, sharp jabs of pain in your groin.

Such pain is harmless. It does not signify injury to you or your baby. But the pain is there and it's scary, and it usually results from a quick forward movement of the abdomen. It can happen when you sneeze or cough or vomit or laugh too hard. It can also happen if you sit up too straight or too quickly.

You can avoid that last cause of round ligament pain if you remember a couple of things. First, never do full sit-ups (which are also hard on the lower back); instead do halfway-up sit-ups (see #23). Second, roll to your side before getting up from a lying down position or before you go from a sitting to a lying position. And third, bend over—quick!—if you feel any twinges of pain.

CIRCULATORY CHANGES

Most of us are not even aware of many of the circulatory changes occurring during pregnancy. For example, you are probably not conscious of the fact that your body now contains between 25 and 45 percent more blood than it did before you became pregnant. But there are some things that happen with pregnancy and circulation that cry out loud and clear.

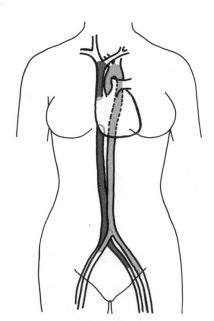

Placement of vena cava and aorta in the pelvis. *Drawing by Tony Fanning*

Take sluggish circulation in the legs for example. As your uterus enlarges, it tends to compress the major veins in your pelvis that carry blood out of your legs and back to your heart. This compression can lead to increased pressure within the veins, and all that, combined with the force of gravity, can lead to the pooling of blood in your legs—the blood just doesn't get out of your legs as efficiently as it should. That, in turn, can lead to aching legs and varicose veins, and dizziness and anxiety too.

Aching Legs. Legs ache and throb when blood is moving sluggishly within their veins. As you know, your heart's job is to pump blood throughout your body. But it needs help, and its helpers are the muscles. Muscles act as auxiliary pumps, and by squeezing against veins, they help move blood back to your heart.

You can temporarily relieve aching legs by using those auxiliary pumps. Never stand still—move instead. Wiggle your toes. Shift your weight. Make ankle circles. Dance a quiet little jig. But *don't* just stand still—your muscles can't help pump blood when they are not being used.

Take daily walks to keep your auxiliary pumps firm and strong—they make better pumps that way. And the walking action helps move blood up and out of your legs.

Whenever possible, elevate your legs and make gravity your ally instead of your foe. If your legs are higher than your pelvis, gravity will help blood move out of your legs and into your torso.

A good rule regarding aching legs is this: Never stand if you can sit (preferably with your feet up), but if you must stand, *move*.

Varicose Veins. Varicose veins can occur in many places, but are generally found in the surface veins of the legs, close to the skin. There they can be seen clearly as knotty purple or dark blue lumps.

Many of the factors that contribute to aching legs also contribute to varicose veins: compression of major veins, increased pressure in the veins, the force of gravity.

But unlike normal veins, varicose veins have lost their tone. The following diagrams will show you what happens.

Veins have valves that open in the direction of the blood flow—always toward the heart. The valves stay open until their pockets fill with blood. *Drawing by Tony Fanning*

When the pockets are full of blood the valves close. This prevents backflow of blood and keeps it moving toward the heart. *Drawing by Tony Fanning*

Varicose veins occur in veins that have lost their tone, and when there is increased pressure in the veins. The increase in pressure causes them to dilate. Dilation impairs the valves' ability to close completely, and there is backflow of blood. Blood then tends to move much more slowly from the legs to the heart. The blood also tends to pool in the pockets, causing stagnation of the blood. *Drawing by Tony Fanning*

Varicosities are sometimes attributable to heredity. But pregnancy, obesity, tight garters or girdles, pelvic tumors, or inflammation of the veins also add to the problem: All these things can cause increased pressure within the veins.

In order to relieve the discomfort of varicose veins, you can do all the things that you can do for aching legs. But, in addition, you should wear elastic stockings or bandages; these will force the blood out of the surface veins of your legs and into the deeper ones.

Many women find that varicose veins are no longer a problem once they have their babies. If you take good care of your legs during pregnancy, you will probably find yourself among those women who do not experience postpartum varicosities.

Dizziness. Dizziness generally occurs because the brain is receiving insufficient oxygen. During pregnancy, many women find that they become dizzy when they have been standing still too long or when they rise too quickly.

During your exercise sessions you will not be standing still, so you should not experience dizziness as a result of *that*. But you will be doing exercises that require your head to be low. So be certain to rise slowly; allow the blood to catch up with your upward movement. Focusing on something as you rise generally helps too. If you find that you are still dizzy once you are upright, sit down and put your head between your legs. This will allow gravity to help the blood flow to your brain.

Anxiety when Supine. Occasionally pregnant women experience anxiety or dizziness when lying on their backs. This occurs because babies compress those major veins that come from the legs and run, parallel to the spine, back to the heart. This compression impedes the flow of blood from the lower extremities and pelvic area to the heart and brain.

You can prevent this simply by lying on your side instead of your back.

FATIGUE

The first trimester of pregnancy is normally a slow, sleepy one. This tiredness is your body's way of telling you that it needs more rest to adapt to pregnancy.

If you continue to experience undue fatigue after the end of your third month (give or take a couple of weeks), you should tell your doctor. Then, after examination, if there is no medical reason for this fatigue, you will probably find that adequate sleep and naps, coupled with regular exercise, increases your energy level. (Take a careful look at your eating patterns too.)

One thing is certain though. Pregnant women simply do not have the stamina and reserve that nonpregnant women have. Bodies must work hard to make a baby, much energy goes into the effort, and so there is not much energy left over.

This, of course, has implications for your exercise program. While moderate exercise can actually give you more energy, overexertion will leave you exhausted. So don't overexert. There is simply no point in pushing too hard; you won't become fitter any faster, and you *will* be tired, sore, and discouraged. Do only as much as *feels good*.

Daily naps during pregnancy give your body the additional rest it needs to do its tremendous work. Unfortunately, many pregnant women, thoroughly indoctrinated by our national work ethic, feel guilty about taking naps. Naps are kissing kin to slothfulness—right? Wrong! Naps are important during pregnancy. Respect your body's need for extra rest and take those naps whenever you feel tired.

STOMACH-BACK RELATIONSHIP

People with strong abdominal muscles generally have strong backs as well. And people with weak abdominals almost always have back problems. That is because your stomach muscles and your back muscles work as a team. And so, even though your stomach muscles are the most visibly affected member of that team, your back muscles are also very much involved in your pregnancy.

Pregnancy tends to increase the natural curvature of the spine, especially during the last trimester. Ideally, your abdominal muscles compensate for this by being strong enough to support the increasing weight and bulk of your baby and to keep your pelvis in alignment. If, however, your abdominals are weak, your back muscles must pitch in to help. Back muscles, however, are not designed to support such weight, and when they must, the result is painfully obvious—your back aches and aches.

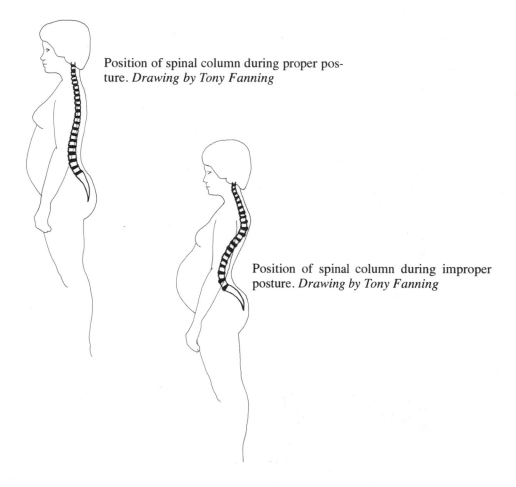

Position of spinal column during proper posture. *Drawing by Tony Fanning*

Position of spinal column during improper posture. *Drawing by Tony Fanning*

Improper posture compounds the problem, especially if you habitually stand with your knees locked and your back swayed. (See chapter 3 on posture.) Standing this way not only greatly increases the strain on your lower back muscles (which leads to backaches), but it makes it virtually impossible to tighten front abdominals (that makes for potbellies).

A good exercise program can help a great deal. By strengthening your abdominal muscles and strengthening and stretching your back muscles, you can do a lot to avoid the discomfort of backaches—now, while you are pregnant, or, for that matter, any time in life. By strengthening postural muscles you can retrain your body to carry itself correctly. All of this can do wonders in preventing backaches, and in improving your appearance.

3

Proper Posture

*W*hen I was a kid, I was told to stand up straight—or else! If I became surly and slumped in rebellion, I was promptly whacked right between the shoulder blades, or threatened with a posture brace, a horrid contraption almost certainly developed in damp, smelly, medieval torture chambers. And so, in fearful obedience, I stood up straight and tall, mostly, as I understood it then, so that I would look pretty.

It wasn't until I was well into college anatomy courses that I discovered that there was more to proper posture than just looking pretty. I learned that improper posture could actually damage an otherwise very fine body—shorten muscles here, weaken or stretch muscles there, stretch or shorten ligaments and tendons in *all* the wrong ways.

And since I've been teaching prenatal fitness classes, I have discovered a couple more things about posture. First, that many of pregnancies' "normal" aches and pains—backaches, low groin discomfort, etc.—can be greatly relieved by standing and sitting properly. And, second, that terrible posture undermines *any* exercise program. Think about it for a minute: It makes perfect sense. If you slump around for sixteen hours each day (112 hours a week), how much good are your two weekly hours of exercise going to do? Besides that, my grandmother was right. Slouchy people *don't* look as attractive as people who stand up tall and proud.

The following photographs will show you what I'm talking about.

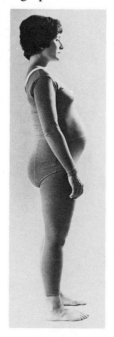

Compare the first two photographs. Can you *believe* that the same body can look so different? But what's even worse than Carol's appearance in that first illustration is what is happening to her body.

There, Carol's posture is contributing to backaches, low groin pain, and aching legs; not to mention sagging breasts, a potbelly, a spreading fanny, and flabby thighs.

Notice that Carol's knees are hyperextended (locked). That impedes blood flow to and from the lower legs, and contributes to blood pooling in the calf area, and to aching legs.

Hyperextension of the knees usually leads to hyperextension of the pelvis. You can see that here. Carol's fanny is protruding, and her lower back is in swayback position. This makes it impossible for her pelvis to act as a cradle for her growing baby. Instead, the baby's bulk (as well as the other abdominal contents) spills forward, pushing against the front abdominal muscles. This kind of pressure contributes to groin pain. But it also leads to backaches, for in this position it is impossible for the abdominal muscles to support the baby's weight. So they holler for help, and the back muscles leap to the rescue. But, try as they might, lower back muscles are just not cut out to substitute for the abdominals, and when they attempt it the result is usually a strained, aching lower back. This swayback position also contributes to loss of muscle tone in the belly, the fanny, and the backs of the thighs. It makes it difficult to keep the muscles in the buttocks and upper/back thighs slightly tensed, and they become weak and flabby. And it is virtually impossible to keep the abdominal muscles tight; the result is usually a potbelly.

Now look at Carol's chest and shoulders. By allowing her shoulders to slump forward she is weakening the muscles between her shoulder blades, which should pull her shoulders back. She is also contributing to tight, shortened pectoral muscles. This all leads to rounded shoulders and a sagging bust line. If this posture is maintained throughout life, it can also lead to "dowagers' hump," an unattractive fatty deposit right where the neck meets the shoulders.

As you can see, poor posture affects more than just your appearance; it can actually create conditions that are damaging to your body. To undo the damage, you must retrain your body to stand properly, and strengthen postural muscles, abdominal muscles, and lower back muscles as well.

But before you can practice good posture, you must understand what it is. Look at the second photograph again. There Carol is standing properly.

Her knees are loose and relaxed, circulation is thereby enhanced, and she is not weakening the muscles needed to keep her knees in proper alignment.

Her pelvis is tipped forward, allowing her to tuck her bottom under and tighten her buttocks and abdominal muscles. This will provide needed support for her baby and abdominal contents, will help prevent low backaches, will help keep her belly muscles strong, and will help keep her buttocks and upper/back thighs from becoming weak and flabby.

Her shoulders are pulled back, but relaxed, and her chest is high. This keeps the postural muscles in the upper back strong enough to keep shoulders back, and it prevents shortening of the pectoral muscles. It also helps prevent drooping breasts.

Her chin is high and her head is in proper alignment. This helps prevent neck aches, sagging jawlines, and—in middle age—dowagers' humps.

It is equally important to sit correctly. All of us love to slump into an easy chair occasionally, and there is no reason to forego that delicious luxury entirely. But, if slumping into chairs is your *primary* way of sitting, watch out. You are again contributing to weakness and discomfort.

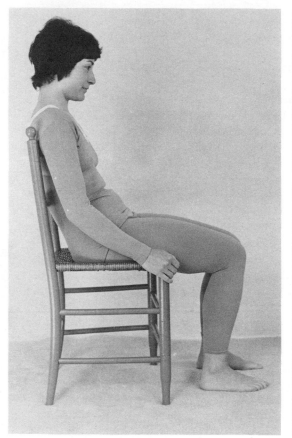 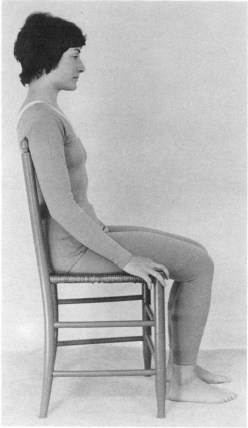

In the first photograph, Carol is sitting improperly. Her pelvis is tipped so that she is resting on the back of it. This causes all the abdominal contents to push against the spine and lower back muscles, leading to weakened muscles and low back strain. Her belly is loose and flaccid; potbellies are born this way. Her upper back is rounded and her middle back is unsupported. Her breasts are drooping and, once again, her chin is jutting forward.

In the second photograph, Carol is sitting properly. Notice that her pelvis is directly beneath her shoulders. She is sitting squarely upon her "sitting bones." (You can find them by sitting on a hard surface and wiggling around until you feel them.) She has pulled her spine straight up from her "sitting bones," and it is in perfect alignment. That means there is no unnecessary stress on any of her back muscles, and her belly remains slightly tensed to keep her there. Her shoulders are comfortably back, and her head is in proper alignment.

I hope these illustrations* help you understand why proper posture is so very important. It may be the best preventative measure there is against all *sorts* of aches and pains; it allows us to get maximum benefit from any exercises we do.

*This set of photographs was taken when Carol was five months postpartum (after delivery).

4
Calisthenics

I can't even count the times that women have asked me, "What about housework? Isn't that exercise?"

And I always answer, "Sure. Some. Especially if you *make* it into exercise. Don't mount the nearest stool to retrieve Jell-O boxes from that almost-too-high shelf. S-t-r-e-t-c-h instead. Same with picking up Suzie's Lego blocks (pegged blocks—a fantastic toy). Don't take the easy way out and crawl around on your hands and knees. Bend from your hips instead (stomach tight, knees loose) to gather those darned things. Might as well get in some hip and hamstring stretching while you're at it. Or else pick them up with your bare ("Prehensile," my husband clucks) toes—great for feet—especially flat ones. Try walking tiptoe from the front of the house to the back, and then goose-step all the way back, arms swinging and legs kicking as high as you can. Canter up any stairs you happen to find, or take them slowly, two at a time to strengthen hips and thighs. Swing your legs as far to the sides as you can as you move forward. Do pelvic floor contractions as you do the dishes. Push that broom with vigor. Scrub the shower or the kitchen floor as if you were going to rid the world of sin and evil once and for all. Wring out the dishrag until you have flushed out the last reluctant drop of water. Turn on some good, loud, four-beat music and boogie as you make the windows shine. Throw in a few roll-ups (#11) for your belly and some wall push-ups (#13) for your shoulders, and—*voilá*—a tailor-made calisthenic program that lets you get that horrible housework done at the same time.

Moral: Housework *can* be exercise if you do it vigorously. Dance! Move! Have fun! (Well . . . maybe asking you to have *fun* is a little too much to hope for.)

"Why then," these women ask me, "should we do anything else? Calisthenics, for instance?"

And I reply, squinty-eyed with what I hope is a penetrating stare, "Because, if you are really, painfully, no-foolin' around *honest* with yourself, you probably will have to admit that you don't *do* most of that stuff long enough or regularly enough to have it count."

"And because your body probably needs to move more than that. And because by pledging yourself to a regular calisthenics program you are guaranteeing yourself that you will *move*. And move properly so that your body will be strong and flexible *all over*. That's why."

"But I *hate* calisthenics," one woman will moan.

"Me too," I reply. "At least I *did* when I started them. When my body had forgotten how to move, and balked at trying, and protested when I *did* try, I *loathed* them."

"But calisthenics become easier and more fun the more you do them," I continue with complete honesty—honestly! "That slug that is your body can relearn movement, and as your body becomes stronger and more limber it will actually *like* moving. And then calisthenics are more fun and actually feel *good*."

"Oh, sure," they mutter with blank stares.

"Honest!"

"Okay—we'll give it a whirl," they say. But they remain unconvinced, I can tell.

However, a few weeks later, their skeletal muscles stronger and more elastic, they begin to understand what I mean. And sometimes they come to me crowing (*this* is what makes teaching so worthwhile), things like:

"I did ten roll-ups today. I couldn't even do two when I started."

Or, "My husband can't believe it—here I am eight months pregnant and I hiked to the *top* of Mount Diablo and wasn't even winded."

Or, "I feel so much better. Since I've been exercising my back doesn't ache anymore."

Once, a lovely woman—forty-two and pregnant with her fifth child—said something to me that made my entire week: "You know, my oldest child is seventeen and my youngest is nine. And even as ancient as I am I have *never* felt this good during pregnancy. I'm *sure* that it's the exercise that's made the difference."

So there you are. Calisthenic exercises—regularly and carefully done—can make your skeletal muscles stronger and more elastic. They help you become more limber, and will strengthen your body all over. They firm you up and slim you down, and can make an astonishing difference in the way you look. They can help you feel better and can help rid your body of aches and pains. And they can help make your delivery *ever* so much easier. They are *great* for you.

But, even so, they are not enough; no *one* type of exercise is. Calisthenics work on that part of you that you see in the mirror. But they don't contribute much to increased stamina and endurance, and they don't do much for those important internal organs that, in the end, keep you *alive:* your heart, your blood vessels, and your respiratory muscles. To get to *those,* to give them better tone and more strength, to make it possible for them to work more easily and efficiently, to build up stamina and reserve, you need *aerobic* exercises.

5
Aerobics

*I*f you're not already familiar with the the concept of aerobic exercise, surely you've wondered what in the world it is.

Aerobic exercise is not calisthenics. Or slimnastics. Or isometrics. Or yoga. Or working with weights. It is swimming, jogging, walking, biking, rowing, dancing, etc. Aerobic exercises differ from other types because aerobics concentrates upon your heart, your lungs, your circulatory system, while the others concentrate upon your musculoskeletal system.

Aerobic exercises are not new, of course. They've been around in one form or another since man loped along prehistoric prairies in search of breakfast. But as a formal exercise concept, aerobics is relatively new. It was Kenneth Cooper who, in the sixties, did the original research on aerobic exercise. It was his premise that in order to become fit one must work with the cardiovascular system, and he established a point system that he believed would lead to cardiovascular fitness. The world of exercise physiology will be forever indebted to Cooper for his findings, which encouraged thousands of otherwise sedentary Americans to get out and move. But recent research indicates that there were a couple of flaws in his basic premises. For one thing, he did not provide for work with skeletal muscles beyond that of the aerobic exercise. It is now pretty universally accepted that aerobics is not enough—in and of itself—to provide total fitness. Skeletal muscles must be stretched and strengthened as well, and that's where calisthenics come in. For another thing, Cooper assumed that the faster you went and the farther you went, the more fit you would become. But speed and distance in something like jogging or walking are only external measures of performance. They tell you nothing about how *your* body is reacting to the exercise. So now pulse-rated exercise is considered to be a safer, more reliable way of becoming cardiovascularly fit. Simply by taking your pulse you will be able to tell exactly how your body is reacting to any physical exertion. (We'll get more into pulses and the value of taking them later in this chapter.)

But for now, a simple definition of aerobic exercise is in order. Any exercise that (a) makes your heart work harder than normal for a longish period of time, while (b) causing your body to demand more oxygen, and (c) making you breathe more deeply and rapidly and use all your lung space—way down to the bottom of your lungs—in the process can be considered an aerobic exercise.

Why bother with aerobic exercise? Because, as I mentioned earlier, it strengthens your heart muscle, it increases your stamina and endurance, it will give you more energy and reserve, it burns lots of calories, it helps trim your figure, and it is absolutely necessary if you want to achieve total fitness.

Whenever you exercise aerobically several things happen.

Since your muscles are actively working for a long period of time they demand more oxygen to sustain the work.

This makes your heart beat faster to supply oxygen-laden blood to those needy muscles.

Your heart is a muscle, and like any other muscle, it becomes weak and flabby if it doesn't receive proper exercise. By pumping faster, as it does during aerobic exercise, it is doing its own version of calisthenics. And, if that exercise is done long enough and continuously enough, your heart becomes stronger. When it's stronger it beats fewer times each minute and is able to rest longer between beats. During each rest period, then, it can fill more completely with blood. With that greater amount of blood inside, the heart's muscle fibers must push against greater pressure as they contract to expel the blood. This strengthens those muscle fibers, makes them work together more efficiently, enables them to expel more blood with each beat, and to expel it more forcefully.

(Those rest periods I mentioned are important for your heart. Let me illustrate why. When I am not regularly jogging, my pulse rate is about 85 beats per minute. When I am jogging regularly, it hovers around 60 beats per minute [except for the actual jogging time when, of course, it is elevated]. That means that as long as I jog my heart is saved 25 beats each minute. And 1,500 beats each hour. And 36,000 beats each day. 13,140,000 beats each year. And if I jog for the next thirty-five years, my heart will *not* have to beat the 459,900,000 times it would have to beat if I didn't jog.)

Your heart's job is to pump blood throughout your body via the blood vessels. Arteries, thick-walled muscular vessels, receive the oxygenated blood and carry it throughout the arterial system to all parts of the body. The arteries become progressively smaller and eventually merge with capillaries. Capillaries are thin-walled tubes just one cell layer thick, so that they can actually accommodate the transfer of oxygen, other nutrients and wastes in the body tissues, and of oxygen and carbon dioxide in the lungs. The capillaries eventually merge with small veins, which merge with larger ones. And then the venous system returns the blood to the heart and the entire process starts over again.

Aerobic exercise improves the tone of the blood vessels, and makes them more pliable, so that they can perform their function more efficiently. And it does something even more astonishing. It can actually cause your body to open latent blood vessels and to create new ones. If your muscles need more oxygen than your body is able to supply, your body will find a way to meet that extra demand. And it does it by opening closed vessels or manufacturing additional blood vessels, so that there are more routes to get the blood where it's needed. This is important for people who have impeded circulation. (Are your hands or feet often cold and/or numb? Usually impeded circulation!) Or where fatty deposits have clogged blood vessels. This is why moderate aerobic exercise is so important for people with high cholesterol counts. The exercise enables your body to break down fatty deposits more readily so that they don't gum up your blood tubes and so that they are more easily absorbed by the body.

Aerobic exercise also improves your lung function. Physical exertion causes us to breathe faster and deeper than normal. That enables us to bring greater quantities of oxygen into our bodies so that the blood can take it to the muscles that need it. This change in breathing pattern causes your lungs to expand more fully. That expansion, in turn, exercises the intercostal muscles between your ribs. As those muscles become stronger and more elastic, they stretch and contract more fully, enabling your lungs to expand to their fullest, so that you bring in and force out more air with each breath. All the time that this is going on, something else really amazing is happening too. All of those tiny little air sacs that line your lungs and that are responsible for facilitating the transfer of oxygen to the bloodstream open up again. Most of us don't use our lungs' full capacity for breathing unless we are physically active. So many of the little air sacs, never really needed, just close up. Once those air sacs are needed once again, as they are during aerobic exercise, they open up happily. And, if necessary, new air sacs are born. So, aerobic exercise can be a real help to people with certain kinds of breathing problems.

What do all these aerobic training effects have to do with your pregnancy? For one thing, they will help you feel better while you're pregnant by giving you more pep. You see, when your heart, lungs, and circulatory systems are working well, your body does not have to use so much energy for those basic functions. And so, there is more energy left for the other things you want to do. But, what is perhaps more important is what aerobics will do for you during labor and delivery. When your cardiovascular system is healthy, when your oxygen delivery system is good, and your lungs strong, your body is much more capable of working hard without tiring. And labor, of course, is hard work. Aerobically fit women labor more efficiently and feel better after delivery than do unconditioned women. It's as simple as that.

But we haven't yet talked about how aerobics helps in weight control programs. Because aerobic exercises are vigorous ones, they burn lots of calories. Slow walking burns about 170 calories an hour. Brisk walking burns close to 300 calories in that same hour. In an hour of easy biking, you'd burn off about 190 calories; bike rapidly and you burn closer to 400 calories. Moderate running burns a good 700 calories an hour, while swimming (freestyle) burns a whopping 1,500. So, if you exercise aerobically and don't increase your food intake, you'll gradually lose weight.

Besides that, aerobics firms and tones all the muscles throughout your body. And that leads to a better looking body.

But how do you know whether the aerobics are really working, whether or not your heart, lungs, and circulation are, in fact, improving?

Your body has a built-in handy little gadget that will let you know at any given point exactly how your body is reacting to exercise, and, over a longer period of time, whether you're really obtaining aerobic training effects. That handy little gadget is your pulse.

Your pulse beat is not the same as your heartbeat. Your pulse is the result of your heartbeat. Each time your heart beats it expels blood into your major arteries. From there it travels throughout your arterial system. And when you feel a pulse beat, what you are feeling is blood surging through an artery that is close to the skin's surface.

Your pulse beat can tell you many things about your body. It tells you how you are reacting to exercise, or to emotional input. It tells you how fast you are using energy—something about your body's metabolic system.

Your pulse count will typically be lowest in the morning after you have awakened from six or more hours of sleep. It rises during the day because you are more active. Any activity—from eating to letter writing to basketball—will make your pulse rate rise. So will many other things. Fever, for example. Or any other increase in body temperature. So will anger or other strong emotions. Deconditioning. And drinking caffeinated beverages. Or smoking. So your pulse tells you a great deal about how your body is functioning.

Your pulse can also tell you about your physical fitness. And generally speaking, the fitter you are, the lower your pulse rate. While there are some physical conditions that result in pulse rates as low as 30 beats a minute or as high as 100 or more beats, most women have a normal resting pulse of somewhere between 75 and 80 beats per minute. Pregnant pulses are more erratic, and it's not uncommon for a pregnant woman's pulse rate to vary a great deal within any given day, or from one day to another. But no matter how low or high your pulse rate is, it is to your benefit to lower it.

During aerobic exercise your pulse rate is always a good index of your body's reaction to the exercise. If your pulse rate is very high, you know that you are working too hard and that you will tire quickly. If it is too low, you are not working hard enough to gain aerobic training effects.

But how do you know when you are working at just the *right* level of exertion? By computing your Safe Heart Rate (SHR) per minute and then figuring out your 15-second "target" pulse count. Your SHR represents the number of times your heart can beat safely each minute during exercise and still benefit aerobically. Your target pulse count is an easy way to keep tabs on your level of exertion. You will find the formula for computing safe SHR and target pulses later in chapter 8.

But first, you should be able to take an accurate pulse count. There are many pulses that you can use, including the ones at your temple, your wrist, or your neck. The one I prefer to use is the carotid artery. This artery is located in the side/front of your throat, right next to your windpipe. Because it is close to your heart, it is virtually impossible to miss after exercise. You can feel it on both sides of your throat. But you'll want to take it on *one* side at a time. If you compress both sides of your carotid artery simultaneously, you can impede your brain's sole supply of blood. People faint that way. Also, never take your pulse with your thumb. There's also a pulse in your thumb, and it's easy to get confused as to which you're counting—the beats of your thumb pulse or those of your carotid artery.

Try to find your carotid artery right now. Using your index and middle fingers, press firmly against your throat, right next to your windpipe. Feel that thumping? No? Then stand up and hop gently from one foot to the other for about two minutes and try again. Now do you feel it? Good. *That* is your carotid artery pulsing.

As you become more fit, you will notice some changes in your pulse. It won't thump as many times each minute (that's because your heart is resting more). It will feel stronger and more forceful. Your arteries will feel thicker, but still soft. And it will be easier to find your pulse, even when you're resting.

You don't have to train like an Olympian to receive aerobic benefits. Anything that puts a slight overload on the heart—makes it beat slightly faster for a while—will work. If you're in poor shape, walking or waltzing might do the job. If you're in good shape, you may have to jog or boogie. But whatever you do, if you do it regularly (at least three times a week for twenty minutes each time), your condition will improve. Within four to six weeks you'll notice that your pulse count is slightly lower than it was when you started, and that you'll have more energy. You'll feel better after your workouts than you did before, and that good feeling will last most of the day. A real tangible benefit of aerobic exercise is feeling more alive and less tired.

6
Exercise Tips Worth Remembering

One thing that I hate about exercise books is that they are frequently so full of rules that if the rules themselves don't scare the liver out of you, they are enough to make you take up tatting instead of jogging. And, yet, I find myself bound by a sense of duty to include my own set of rules. Please read them. I'm including them only because I really think they are important.

1. *Before you begin, get medical approval.*

   You really should have a thorough medical examination (including a resting electrocardiogram [ECG] if you're between thirty and thirty-nine, and an ECG taken during exercise if you are over forty), and obtain your doctor's approval for your exercise program before you begin *any* fitness program. This precautionary measure is important for three reasons.

   First, your doctor is usually the best judge of your state of health. Women experiencing normal, uncomplicated pregnancies can benefit greatly from a good, regular program of exercise. However, exercise is not always recommended for women experiencing abnormal pregnancies. Your doctor will be able to make the best judgment about you and your pregnancy in relation to exercise.

   Second, physical fitness cannot be fully achieved if you are hampered by correctable physical defects ("bad" knees that result from weak muscles or improper footwear, for example). Let your doctor help you create a good therapeutic exercise program to correct such defects so that you can attain a good level of fitness.

   Third, it's important for your own peace of mind. In many cultures it is taken for granted that pregnant women will remain physically active. Unfortunately, our culture has done an outstanding job of convincing most of us that pregnancy should be a passive rather than an active time. So it is very normal to wonder about the effects of exercise upon your pregnancy. It is tremendously reassuring to have the support of your physician. If you are going to exercise, I'd suggest finding a physician who knows something about exercise and its effects. Many don't. Try to find someone who exercises him/herself.

2. *Go at your own rate of endurance.*

   This is one of the most fundamental exercise principles. It is *crucial* that you respect your body's capabilities and not push too hard. You can trust your body to tell you when it has had enough or when it wants more. Listen to your body. Respect its messages.

Unfortunately, many of us become impatient with our bodies. We want to do more than we really should. It takes several years to become truly unfit. And so it makes sense to assume that it will take a while to get back in shape. There can be a problem when we see someone finishing her forty-fifth sit-up in the time it has taken us to squeeze out nine, and we think that if we only push harder we can catch up; or we remember when, on the high school swimming team, we could swim eighty laps without stopping, and somehow forget that ten years of inactivity have passed since then; or we realize that the baby is due in only four months, so we'd better beat ourselves into shape—fast. Therefore, we sometimes work too hard, are never quite satisfied with our performance, experience extreme fatigue, aching muscles, and perhaps even injure ourselves. It's simply not worth it. And it doesn't work anyway.

So relax. Go just as slowly as you need to, but *keep going,* always at your own rate, your own speed. Time is on your side. Keep working and fitness will come.

3. *Exercise regularly.*

Irregular exercise is potentially more harmful than no exercise at all. The woman who neglects her exercise for a month, and then tries to do what she could have done a month before, often pushes too hard and may hurt herself. So if you are going to exercise, you must promise yourself that you will do it at least three times a week on nonconsecutive days. Only through regular exercise can you achieve a good level of fitness and avoid strain or injury.

Another thing that you should know about fitness is that it can disappear. It is not like eating too much food and having your body store the excess. If you do not exercise regularly, you will lose the fitness level you have worked so hard to gain, or you will not become fit in the first place. That's not a pleasant fact. But fact it is.

4. *Take care of your health.*

It's possible to be healthy (disease-free) and unfit. But it's impossible to be fit and not healthy. Your good health is your most valuable resource, so treat it with the same respect and care that you would Aunt Matilda's fine china. Get plenty of rest, eat good, nourishing foods (be certain that your diet during pregnancy includes lots of protein and iron-laden foods), and, of course, exercise moderately and regularly.

5. *Stop if you feel pain.*

Pain is not the same thing as underused muscles asserting themselves by aching. Pain is your body's way of telling you that something is wrong. If you experience pain during any exercise, stop that exercise at once and don't do it again until you have consulted your doctor. Chances are that the pain is telling you that you have one of those correctable defects that needs correcting before you continue the exercises, or that you've pushed too hard. Your doctor is the one to make those decisions and to help you modify your exercise program to meet *your* body's needs.

Pain is one distress signal. There are others: dizziness, seeing spots, nausea, chest pain, difficult breathing, loss of muscle control. If any of these signals crop up, contact your doctor.

6. *Take your time.*

You'll get much more out of your exercise sessions if you let yourself *enjoy* them. Movement is wonderful. So concentrate on that movement and let your daily cares go. But exercise is no fun if you haphazardly try to squeeze it in among dozens of other activities. Give it priority. Set time aside for exercise, and then go slowly enough to really enjoy it. Take your time.

7. *Do the exercises properly.*

You can't be sloppy about exercise and derive desired results. Sloppiness leads to incorrect use of your body and your muscles and it perpetuates those bad body habits that you're trying to shake. All that leads to decreased exercise benefits.

So before you do any exercise (including walking and jogging), please read the instructions for that exercise. Try the exercise. Reread the instructions to make sure that you did it correctly. Then try it again, paying careful attention to how your body feels when it is working properly. Keep trying to do it properly, and before you know it, correct movement will become automatic.

8. *Drink water.*

It is important to maintain an adequate fluid level in your body when you exercise. Without sufficient fluid, your body becomes slow to react and easily fatigued. So drink water whenever you feel the need while you are exercising; it will help replace the fluid you have lost through exertion. It's best to keep your water intake to frequent doses of six to eight ounces rather than one long drink of two or three cups.

9. *Always warm up.*

It is important to warm up at the first of each exercise session and before you walk or jog. Joint warm-ups (#s 1–5) prepare the joints for more strenuous exercise by causing the synovial membranes in the joints to secrete synovial fluid, a joint lubricant, and by causing joint connective tissue to become thicker and shorter, and therefore stronger. They also help related muscle areas become ready for more strenuous exercise. All this lessens the likelihood of strain or injury to the joint areas and related tissues.

10. *Always cool down.*

Cool downs are important because they bring your respiration, your heart rate, and your metabolism back to near normal.

After calisthenics, you can cool down by doing some gentle slow stretches.

After aerobics, cool down by doing your aerobic exercise, but less vigourously. For example, if you jog, cool down by walking slowly and swinging your arms. The blood vessels in your legs dilate during jogging to meet your muscles' increased oxygen needs. If you just stand still when you finish jogging, it is easy to faint. Gravity, inactive muscles, and dilated veins all team together to help blood pool in your legs. Your brain doesn't receive sufficient oxygen, and you can pass out. So walk, swinging your arms. The arm swinging tells your body that more oxygen is needed upstairs. So enough blood leaves your legs to meet that demand. Walking will also allow your heart rate and breathing to return to normal.

11. *Exhale when you are working hardest.*

It's tempting to hold your breath when you exercise, especially when you are working hard. Holding your breath can cause problems though—it causes your glottis to close. This, in turn, leads to an increase in the pressure in the blood vessels in your torso. That leads to a decrease in the blood returning to your heart. Cardiac output then decreases, and your heart receives less oxygen—just when it needs oxygen most. To prevent this, make a point of exhaling when you are working hardest on each exercise. If you do that, the inhaling will take care of itself.

You can feel your glottis close. Inhale, and once your lungs are full of air, hold your breath. Feel what happens in the back of your throat? That increased pressure is caused by your glottis closing.

12. *Stretches should be long, slow, and gentle.*

Many believe that vigorous bouncing during a stretch is the best way to increase flexibility. Actually, your muscles interpret bounces as threats to their well-being and shorten a bit to protect themselces from injury. This reaction is called the Stretch Reflex, and it does not allow for maximum stretch.

Long, slow, gentle (bounceless) stretches are best, and a good stretch should last from 30 to 60 seconds.

To get a good stretch, gently relax into the stretching position, and, breathing deeply and regularly, hold that position for 20 to 30 seconds. Then gently increase the stretching position as fully as you can *without strain*. Continue to breathe deeply and regularly, and hold that increased stretch for another 20 to 30 seconds. Gently come out of the stretch.

Stretches done this way will decrease the likelihood of muscle strain, and—done regularly—will result in good flexibility.

13. *Bend to the sides before you bend forward.*

When you bend forward (for example, when you touch your toes), your spinal muscles have a tendency to stretch unevenly unless they are first warmed up. So, do lateral bends (#7) before you bend forward.

It works this way. As you bend to one side, the muscles on the longest side of your trunk and spine stretch, while those on the shortest side are in a state of relative relaxation. As you bend to the other side, the process is reversed. After you have warmed up this way, you can go ahead and bend forward.

The same principle applies to necks. Work laterally before you bend your head forward or do neck rolls.

14. *Work on a firm, but soft surface.*

Spines and joints can be bruised if you work on a hard surface. So work on grass instead. Or a carpet. Or a foam exercise mat. (Instructions for making one are on pages 140–41.) Or anything else that will protect your bones.

15. *Pull out after each strenghtening exercise.*

You can avoid a lot of post-exercise discomfort if you take a couple of seconds to pull out after each strengthening exercise.

For example, Modified Push-Ups (#21) are hard work for muscles in your arms, shoulders, and chest. To pull out those muscles, you could bend over from your hips, let your arms and head relax, and swing your arms. Or you could do Shoulder Shrugs (#19). Or you could swing your arms across your chest. Or all of them. You can always make up pullouts. Just find some way to move, or rub, that part of you that is letting you know it's been working.

If you always exercise at your own rate of endurance, and are faithful about pulling out when you feel the need, you will find that you will almost never end up with achy muscles.

16. *Exercise to music.*

It's much more fun, and you'll feel more like a dancer than a drudge. Play any music that you love that makes you feel good inside—from classical to acid rock.

7

Your Regular Calisthenic Exercise Routine

*H*ere is my suggested calisthenic exercise routine. If you don't like it, turn to chapter 9, How to Create Your Own Fitness Program. And then look carefully at chapter 10, Additional Exercises, and pick out some exercises that suit you better.

At the risk of sounding like a preacher, I'd like to caution you on one point.

Your body is a beautifully integrated *whole*. And it's all interconnected. If you exercise only one or two parts of it, you'll be neglecting other parts and thereby creating weak links. And a couple of weak links can spoil the entire chain.

In this regular exercise routine I have provided calisthenics that will use all your major muscle groups, and that will keep you in shape *all over*. Don't neglect *any* of them; they are all important for the *whole* you. There may be some exercises that you don't like or that simply don't *feel* right. Fine. But if you decide to eliminate any of these exercises, turn to chapter 10, select exercises that work on the same muscle groups, and plug them in instead.

You will notice that I haven't told you how many times to *do* each exercise. I *could* arbitrarily tell you to do, say, ten roll-ups each time. They would probably feel like work at first, especially if you hadn't been exercising. That's because you would be overloading your front abdominals which would be working longer and harder than before. But, pretty soon, when your abdominals become stronger, ten roll-ups will seem pretty easy. That happens because your abdominals would be, by that time, *used* to doing ten roll-ups. No longer would they be overloaded. And, instead of becoming increasingly fit, their level of fitness would stabilize.

That principle of overload is the cornerstone of becoming fit: Your body will become more fit only as long as it's working harder than it's used to working. That's overloading; and just a little bit at any one time is fine—too much overload can lead to fatigue and/or injury. So you will want to overload gradually and gently.

There are several ways you can overload safely. One is to do each exercise more times than before. So, if you feel the effort of three roll-ups at first, stick with three. When three roll-ups begin to fell comfortable, do four. And then five, etc.

Or you can do the exercises more often. Instead of exercising three days, you can exercise four. Or instead of just once a day, exercise twice.

Another way is to choose more difficult versions of each exercise. For example, when you've reached the point where you can easily do twenty roll-ups (that's an arbitrary figure), and it doesn't make sense to you to work up to thirty (also arbitrary), you're ready for a more difficult version of the roll-up. I've included more difficult versions of each exercise where I think it's appropriate. Warning: You may find that you're pooped after doing only a few of the more difficult versions of any exercise. Great. That's overload for you. Just go slowly and build up gradually.

Overload applies to aerobics too, of course. And I'll talk more about this in chapter 8, Your Regular Aerobics Program.

One more thing. I know that joint warm-ups can *seem* like a waste of time when what you really want to zero in on is your belly or hips or thighs. But *don't* neglect these warm-ups. They're important for joint lubrication, strengthening joint connective tissue for more strenuous activity, and for preparing related muscle tissue for increased effort. They are *especially* important now that you're pregnant because Relaxin has softened all your joint connective tissue.

And don't forget your aerobics. Good luck!

#1. Neck Rolls

Cautions and Hints: If you have a history of neck problems, go very slowly. Do just one set the first few days, and gradually work up. If your neck is really tight or sore, don't try to push through that soreness. That will only make the soreness worse. Go around the soreness instead. And go *slowly*. This exercise can be very relaxing. Close your eyes and enjoy it.

Benefits: This works with all the muscles in your neck, and with some of the back, chest, and shoulder muscles. It is super for releasing shoulder and neck tension.

Position: Sit on the floor, legs crossed Indian style (tailor position). Let your hands rest comfortably on your legs. Wiggle around until you feel your sitting bones, and then pull your spine into alignment from there. Keep your stomach tight, your back straight, and your shoulders relaxed.

Procedure

1. Let your head fall slowly to the left side, aiming your left ear directly toward your left shoulder.
2. Hold for a count of 5.
3. Slowly lift your head to center.
4. Then allow it to fall slowly to the right side.
5. Hold for a slow count of 5.
6. Repeat steps 1–5 two or three times.
7. Then, slowly allow your head to fall forward, until your chin is close to your throat.
8. Hold for a slow count of 5.
9. Slowly raise your head, loosen your jaws (so that your top teeth don't touch your bottom ones), and—carefully! with control—allow your head to go slowly backward. This movement must be controlled. Your head weighs a lot. If you let that head weight *clunk* backward, you might pull the muscles in the back of your neck.)
10. Repeat steps 7–9 two or three times.
11. Finally, slowly, make big circles with your head. Go first in one direction, then in the other. Make these circles large and slow, so that you can work *all* your neck muscles.

More Difficult: Use your hands to resist the movement, by placing them against your head. As you let your head fall to the left, place your left hand against the left side of your head and push against your head with your hand, at the same time that you push against your hand with your head. And so on. This version is really more for *strengthening* neck muscles.

#2. Arm Circles

Cautions and Hints: If you have a history of shoulder joint problems, go carefully here.

Benefits: This shoulder joint warm-up uses the muscles across the back of your shoulders and neck (trapezius), the muscles on top of your shoulders (deltoids), those in the front (biceps) and back (triceps) and in the inside (quadriceps) of your arms, and your chest muscles (pectorals). It is a good firmer upper of the upper arm.

Position: Sit on the floor in tailor fashion. Keep your back straight, your stomach tight, your head high. Extend your arms straight out to the sides at shoulder level.

Procedure

1. Turn palms up and make small circles with your arms, making the movement come from the shoulder joint.
2. Turn palms down, and continue the small circles. Are you using your *entire* arm, or are you bending at the elbow and using your forearm?
3. Palms up again, and make larger circles.
4. Palms down, and the same larger circles.
5. Now, palms up, and make *very* large circles. Stretch up from your rib cage at the top of each very large circle.
6. Palms down, and repeat the very large circles, with the stretch.
7. Now, repeat the entire sequence, making circles in the opposite direction.

More Difficult: Hold weight bags while you do this. (Instructions for making weight bags are on pages 134–35.)

#3. Hip Joint Warm-ups

Cautions and Hints: Sometimes the pubic symphysis (fibrocartilage that connects the pelvic bones directly above your clitoris) is bothered by exercises involving side leg extensions. If you experience that discomfort, don't allow your leg to go so far to the side. This leaning-back position may bother bad shoulders.

Benefits: This, of course, warms up your hip joints. In addition to that, it is a super thigh firmer, and works on inner, top, and side thigh muscles. It also works on the front abdominal muscles, and the lateral abdominals too.

Position: Sit on the floor. Extend your legs straight out in front of you. Place your hands about 12 inches from your buttocks and lean back on your arms. (If your shoulders are bothered in this position, do Side Leg Lifts [#38] instead.) Keep your belly tight.

Procedure

1. Lift your left leg as high as possible without lifting your right knee off the floor.
2. Swing your left leg all the way over to the right side and touch your foot to the ground.
3. Lift it up again, swing it across your body, and touch your foot to the floor on the left side of your body.
4. Repeat steps 2–3.
5. Now make large circles with your left leg, making the movement come from your hip.
6. Make the same large circles in the opposite direction.
7. Repeat the entire sequence with the right leg.

More Difficult: Use weight bags on your ankles.

#4.   Knee Circles

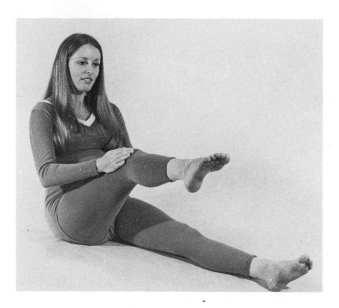

Cautions and Hints: If you place your hands to the *sides* of your knee, your belly will have to work to support the weight of your leg. If you support your knee from *underneath,* your belly will lose all that good work. If you have bad knees, go slowly and carefully.

Benefits: This exercise not only warms up knees, but it is a good firmer upper of extra flab about the knees. It also involves work with the muscles in the front of your thighs, all the muscles around your knees, and your front abdominals.

Position: Sit on the floor, with your back as straight as possible, and your belly tight. Lift your right leg off the floor and bend your knee. Place your hands on either side of that right knee.

Procedure

1. Keeping your right thigh and hip joint as stable as possible, make slow, big circles with your right lower leg. Make the circles come from the knee joint.
2. Now change the direction of the circles.
3. Repeat steps 1—2 with your left leg.

More Difficult: Put weight bags on your ankles.

#5. Ankle Circles

Cautions and Hints: If you have ever sprained your ankle, you may find that it just doesn't want to cooperate during this exercise. Just keep working—slowly—and give it time to relearn movement.

Benefits: When I was a teen-ager and hooked on *Seventeen* magazine, I read that this exercise is supposed to guarantee slender ankles. I'm not sure that I buy that, but I *do* know that besides being a good warm-up for ankle joints, it is a good ankle strengthener. And *that's* good to know if you like to play tennis, go hiking, skating, walk barefoot on the beach or grassy fields, etc. During this exercise, you'll be working with all your ankle muscles, your shin muscles, your top thigh muscles, and your front abdominals.

Position: Sit on the floor, legs extended straight in front of you. Cross your arms *over your belly*. (Don't lean back on them or you'll cheat yourself out of some good belly work.) Keep your back as straight as possible, and keep your belly tight. Lift your right leg 10 inches off the floor, keeping your knee straight.

Procedure

1. Keeping your leg straight, and moving only from the ankle joint, make large, slow circles with your right foot.
2. Make the same large, slow circles in the opposite direction.
3. Repeat steps 1—2 with your left foot.

More Difficult: Tie your weight bag around your foot.

#6. Allover Stretch

Cautions and Hints: Keep your body straight and in good alignment during the first part of this exercise. It's tempting to jut your hips out, but don't do it because you loose good torso stretching that way. For maximum benefit, go *very* slowly.

Benefits: This uses every major muscle group except those below your knees. That's why this is probably the best stretch I know of.

Position: Kneel on your right knee, right foot directly behind your knee. Extend your left leg straight out to the left side, keeping your knee straight but not locked. Raise your right arm, palm facing the ceiling. Place your left hand on your left thigh. Tighten your hips and belly, tuck your fanny under, and pull your body up as tall as you can. (Don't hunch shoulders though.)

Procedure

1. Inhale.
2. As you exhale, keep your hips tight and your shoulders "flat against the wall"; stretch even higher with your right hand, then slowly lean as far to the left as you can without changing the position of your hips.
3. Breathe normally, and stretch your right arm as far as you can, trying to "touch" that distant left-hand wall.
4. Hold that long stretch as you breathe normally and slowly count to 10.
5. Now, release your hips, and round your upper back by rolling your right shoulder a little so that it is aimed toward your left knee.
6. Stretch until you can touch your left foot with your right hand. (Or get as close as possible.)
7. Hold, breathing normally, as you slowly count to 10.
8. Now, keeping your long stretch, slowly lead with your right shoulder and, reversing the movement that brought you down, return to starting position.
9. Then place your right hand on the back of your right calf, close to your ankle.
10. Stretch your left arm over your head, with your upper arm parallel to your ear.
11. "Open" your entire body, so that your belly faces the ceiling and your shoulders are roughly parallel to the floor.
12. Now, stretch as far behind you as you can with your left arm.
13. Hold that stretch and slowly count to 10, breathing normally.
14. Now, try to touch the floor with your left hand. (You'll never make it, of course, but that's the movement you want.)
15. Hold that stretch for a slow count of 10. Breathe!
16. Slowly bring your left arm over your belly and to the right side of your body.
17. Bend your right elbow and allow your body to "roll" to the right.
18. Return to starting position. Kneel on your left knee, and extend your right leg to the side.
19. Repeat steps 1–17 (17!), leaning to the right.

More Difficult: This is *just fine* as it is.

#7. Lateral Bends

Cautions and Hints: This can be stressful on bad lower backs. To minimize lower back strain, hold your front abdominals in hard, tuck your fanny under, and tighten your buttocks. Then, in this position, keep your hips stable, and try to make all movement come from the waistline and above. No jutting of the hips, please!

Benefits: This is a torso trimmer in the truest sense of the word. It works your lateral abdominals and your lateral back muscles. These are the muscles that contour your torso, tuck in your waistline (yes, it's really still *there*), and *hold* in your belly. Want a little middle? Keep this exercise in your daily routine.

Position: Stand upright in proper posture. (Forget what *that* is? Go back to chapter 3.) Place your feet apart for balance. Tuck your fanny under, and tighten your abdomen and buttocks. Raise your right arm above your head, and place your left hand across your belly.

Procedure

1. Stretch your right arm up *as far as possible*. (You should feel your ribs lifting, and your whole right side stretching.)

2. Inhale. Then exhale as you bend to the left, keeping that long stretch. Keep your shoulders flat, as if they were against a wall.

3. Lean as far as possible without readjusting your hips.

4. Lengthen your stretch even more, and hold for a slow count of 5, breathing normally.

5. Then, s-l-o-w-l-y return to starting position. (This should feel like *work*. As you raise your torso, push down a little with the fingers of your left hand, and you can *feel* your lateral abdominals work to raise your body.)

6. Repeat steps 1–4, with your left arm raised, and leaning to the right.

   More Difficult: Clasp your hands behind your neck and do the exercise as instructed. (This is harder on lower backs.)

#8.   Hamstring Stretch

Cautions and Hints: Don't, I repeat, *don't* lock your knees, tempting as it may be. Locked knees not only can lead to knee joint and back problems, but can impede circulation in the lower legs as well. Keep your head relaxed, and chin close to your throat. If you lift your chin, you'll be losing out on some good upper back stretch. And keep your belly *tight*.

Benefits: This stretches the hamstring muscles in the back of your thighs, your calf muscles, your lower back muscles, and your hip flexors. It's a good back relaxer, and if you let yourself relax into this position whenever you feel a backache sneaking up on you, you'll find that those nasty backaches never quite grab you.

Position: Stand upright, feet slightly apart, knees relaxed but straight, belly tight.

Procedure

1. Tuck your chin to your throat, round your back, gently roll down, and try to touch your toes with your fingers. If you can't quite get down to your toes, go only as far as you can without strain.

2. Breathe deeply, and each time you exhale, try to relax through your back, your hips, and your hamstrings. Do this for about 30 seconds.

3. Now, gently increase your stretch by grasping the backs of your calves (as low on your legs as possible) with your hands.

4. And gently pull your body toward your legs.

5. Hold, breathing deeply and trying to relax with each exhalation, for about 30 seconds.

6. Bend your knees, and slowly return to starting position.

More Difficult: Not needed.

#9. Inner Thigh Stretch

Cautions and Hints: Inner thigh muscles are generally tight on people who have previously been nonexercisers. And, if they're pulled, they really *hurt*. So, please go carefully. Again, no locked knees.

Benefits: This stretches the inner thigh muscles. It's a good delivery exercise because it also stretches the pelvic floor, and because tight inner thigh muscles often ache after delivery, especially if delivery stirrups have been used. If these muscles are elastic and can stretch easily, the ache is greatly reduced. Your lower back and hip flexor muscles also get some good stretching.

Position: Stand upright with your feet spread apart as far as possible without strain. Please, don't attempt this in socks or anything else that makes your feet slippery. (No one that I know has ever unwillingly slid into a split from this position, but I keep waiting for it to happen.)

Procedure

1. Keeping your belly tight, gently bend over from your hips as far as you can without strain.
2. Relax your head, shoulders, and arms.
3. Hang for about 30 seconds, breathing deeply, and relaxing with each exhalation.
4. Gently rise to starting position.

More Difficult: Spread your legs further apart. Or, increase the stretch by placing your arms between your legs and "walking" your fingers back through them as far as possible. Then hold *that*.

#10.   Pelvic Tilt

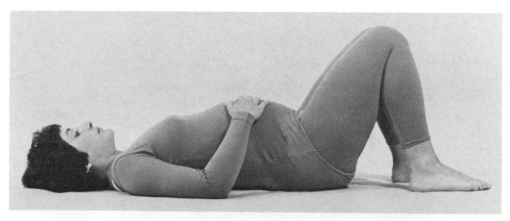

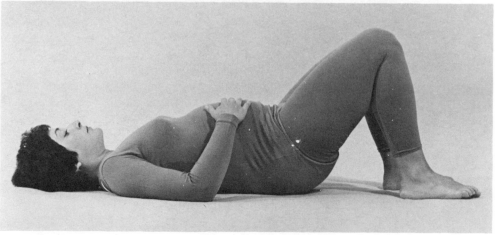

Cautions and Hints: You can see what a tiny movement is involved in this exercise by checking the difference in Carol's buttocks in the photographs. The movement *is* small, but it's effective.

Benefits: This is a good delivery exercise. It strengthens, and contributes to increased flexibility in, the lower back. It firms up front abdominals and pelvic floor muscles too. Plus, it helps your entire pelvic area regain mobility. Good for people with aching backs.

Position: Lie on your back. Bend your knees, and place your feet apart and flat on the floor. Rest your arms wherever they are most comfortable.

Procedure

1. Tighten your buttocks, the backs of your thighs, and your belly.
2. Press your waistline down to the floor. Then lift your tailbone off the floor.
3. Hold as you slowly count to 5. Please breathe.
4. Now, slowly return to starting position. (Don't just collapse—unroll instead.)

More Difficult: Do the Angry Cat (#30) and then Back Tuck and Arch (#31).

#11. Roll-Ups

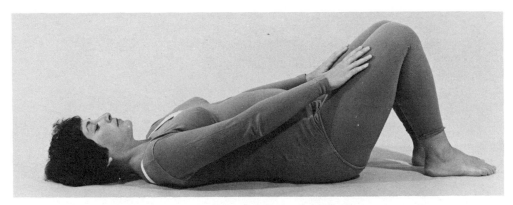

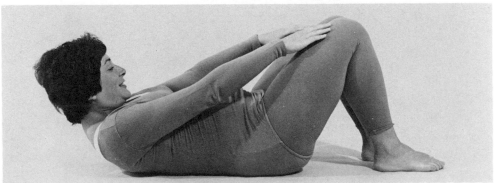

Cautions and Hints: Many people complain of neck discomfort when beginning this exercise. That's because your neck will be *lifting* the weight of your head instead of just *holding* it as usual. Try putting a small pillow or a rolled towel under your head until the neck muscles get stronger. This exercise is not for people with hernias. Holding the position can be potentially harmful for cardiac patients.

Benefits: The thing that makes this such a good exercise for strengthening and firming front abdominals is that, with your knees bent, your belly must work hard to raise your back and hold it in the roll-up position.

Plus, your back is completely supported, so you'll not strain it.

Position: Lie on your back on the floor. Bend your knees and place your feet flat on the floor, slightly apart. Let your hands rest on your thighs.

Procedure

1. Inhale
2. As you exhale, tuck your chin to your throat, roll both shoulders off the floor, and slowly push your hands up your thighs until they are as close to your knees as you can get them without lifting your waistline off the floor.
3. Hold, breathing normally, as you slowly count to 10. As you hold, you'll feel the work start at the top of your abdominal area. As you continue to hold the work moves down into your lower abdominal area too.
4. Slowly and with great control, roll back to starting position.

More Difficult: Clasp your fingers behind your neck when doing the exercise. When that's too easy, raise both arms over your head. If that ever becomes too easy, begin using an incline board to do your roll ups.

#12. Pelvic Floor Strengtheners

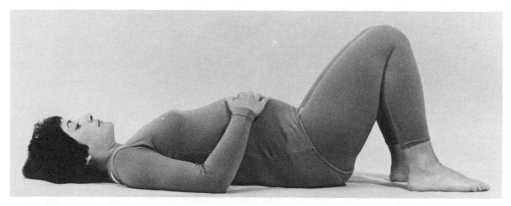

Cautions and Hints: Pelvic floor muscles run right between your legs, and include, among others, the rectal muscles, the vaginal muscles, and the urinary sphincter.

Strong pelvic floor muscles are important during pregnancy; your baby's head rests on them during the last few weeks before delivery. If they are strong, you'll experience less discomfort. It is equally important to be able to *relax* them at will so that your baby's head won't have to push against tightened muscles during delivery. That makes labor longer and more uncomfortable than it need be.

After delivery, pelvic floor muscles are stretched. Then it is important to resume these exercises to increase the blood flow to the perineum (the area between your vagina and your anus), thus promoting healing of the episiotomy incision (the incision in the perineum frequently used during childbirth to prevent tearing of perineal tissue), to tighten vaginal muscles for increased sensation during sexual intercourse, and to help regain greater bladder control.

To find these muscles, try to stop the flow of urine during urination.

A small P.S.: The great thing about this exercise is that it can be done anyplace, and no one even needs to know that you're exercising. I encourage my students to think of a situation that will remind them to do this exercise every time they find themselves in it. Some of my students have used stopping at stoplights to do their pelvic floor strengtheners, or talking on the telephone, or doing dishes, or changing diapers. You can find your own situation. Just be sure that you *do* the pelvic floor exercises when you find yourself there.

Position: As I mentioned before, this exercise can be done in any position. But if you really want to isolate these muscles, you might try this one for starts.

Lie on your back on the floor. Prop your knees together, and place your feet apart. Keep your waistline on the floor and let your legs completely relax. (They should support each other.) Place your hands wherever they are most comfortable. (If you put your fingertips just above your pubic bone and push down hard, you can feel these muscles working.)

Procedure

1. Tighten and relax the pelvic floor muscles.

2. Vary the speed; vary the length of holding.

3. Try to isolate your urinary sphincter (the muscles controlling the urinary tract) and your vaginal muscles. (You can't do this completely, but with practice you'll be able to tell which is which.)

4. Now, pay particular attention to *relaxing* the muscles.

More Difficult: Not needed.

#13. Wall Push-ups

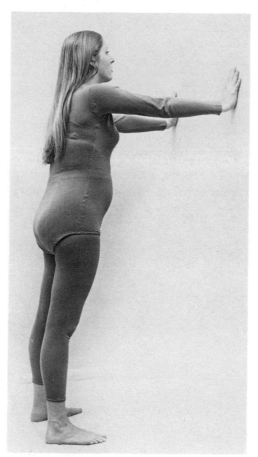 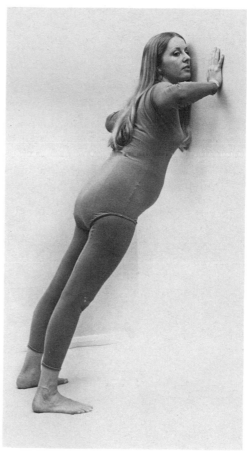

Cautions and Hints: This can be hard on weak or bad shoulders. If you're bothered, go very slowly and build up gradually. Please—no sagging bodies. Keep your body absolutely straight from your heels to your shoulders. Keep your heels on the ground, and your belly tight.

Benefits: All types of push-ups emphasize work with the pectoral muscles in your chest and the triceps muscles in the back of your arms. Besides that, this is a good allover shoulder/upper arm strengthener and firmer, and involves all major shoulder and upper arm muscle groups. By keeping your heels on the floor, you will be stretching calf muscles and Achilles tendons as well. This will prepare your shoulders and arms for carrying that baby *outside* your body. Believe me, a 7-pound baby can seem to weigh *tons*.

Position: Face a wall, with your feet 2 to 3 feet away from the wall. (If you are short, your legs will have to be closer to the wall than if you are tall.) Spread your feet approximately 12 inches apart. Place your hands on the wall at shoulder height, and slightly further apart than your shoulders are wide. Spread your fingers. Keep your abdomen tight, and your body straight from your heels to your shoulders. (No sagging hips allowed.) And keep those heels down.

Procedure

1. With your body straight, inhale as you bend your elbows until your cheek touches the wall.
2. Exhale as you return to starting position.
3. Repeat several times—until you feel the effort of this exercise.

More Difficult: Do Modified Push-Ups (#21). Or, move your feet further away from the wall. When that's too easy, place your hands on a table and do your push-ups that way. Then go to a low bench.

#14. The Doggy

Cautions and Hints: Be careful if you have bad knees or shoulders. That tightening you feel just opposite your hip joint is probably the result of unused muscles letting you know they're still around. (If it's pain that's something else. See your doctor.) Keep your belly tight all the time, and keep your arms straight.

Warning: This exercise is pure *torture*. It has the very dubious benefit of *never* getting easier, no matter *how* much you do it. (I've been doing it for seven years now and it still *kills* me.) The best things that can be said about it are that it works, and it is a surefire way to create a sense of virtuous martyrdom.

Benefits: Oh the benefits! This is a fine thigh and buttocks firmer. It uses all your gluteal muscles (buttocks), and the muscles on the upper side/back of your thigh (right where the saddlebags are).

Position: Rest on your hands and knees. Keep your belly *tight* (otherwise your lower back is going to sway) and your arms straight.

Procedure

1. Bend your right knee as you bring it as close to your right shoulder as possible, and as high as possible.
2. Now, straighten your right leg, keeping it as close to the shoulder line as possible. If your side hip and thigh muscles are weak, you will have to extend it more to the back than to the side. (What's the shoulder line? Pretend that there is a *long* stick touching the front of both your shoulders and extending out to the sides from there. Try to make your foot touch that "stick." *That's* the shoulder line.)
3. Breathing normally, hold for a slow count of 5.
4. Bend your knee again.
5. Bring your leg back to starting position.
6. Repeat steps 1–5 with your left leg.

More Difficult: When you feel strong enough, follow steps 1–3. But instead of returning to starting position, bounce your right leg up (gently, gently) 5 times. Then make 5 large forward circles. Then 5 big backward circles. Then bend and straighten your leg 5 times. Then follow steps 4–6.

8

Your Regular Aerobics Program

*M*ildred Cooper's *Aerobics for Women* or Kenneth Cooper's *Aerobics* and *New Aerobics* contain complete lists of exercises deemed aerobically beneficial. You might want to look through all three books. (See chapter 15 for additional information.)

It doesn't really matter *which* type of aerobic exercise you choose to do, as long as you enjoy it, it feels right, and you do it regularly.

I began jogging seven years ago. And I still jog most of the time. But sometimes when I've had it with jogging, I walk instead. Or I turn on some rock music and dance. All three of these exercises are convenient (you can do them almost anywhere, with or without other people), inexpensive (the only investment you need to make is in good shoes), and fun.

You may want to do something else—swim, or bike, or jump rope (although, personally, I can't *imagine* jumping rope during pregnancy). Whatever type of exercise you choose, remember to do it regularly, to monitor your pulse, and to stay close to your target pulse rate. If you do that, you'll work at a level of exertion that is just right for you. And you'll gain aerobic training effects.

But before you can do that, you have to know what your target pulse rate is. So take time right now figure that out. And take your resting pulse count.

First, take your resting pulse count. Sit down and relax for about 5 minutes. Then find your carotid artery. Watch the second hand on your clock and count your pulse beats for one full minute. What you'll get is a reasonably accurate resting pulse count for one minute. If you want a truly accurate one, take your pulse for one full minute each morning for three days—before you get out of bed. Write down each morning's pulse count. Add these up. Then divide the total by 3. That will give you a very accurate resting pulse count. Whichever method you use, write your resting pulse count down on the calendar next to the date. That way you'll be able to compare it to later resting pulse counts.

Now, figure out your Safe Heart Rate and your target pulse count according to the following formula.

1. First, subtract your age from 220. The resulting number is your Maximum Heart Rate (MHR) for one minute.

2. Now, multiply your MHR by .60. The resulting number is your Safe Heart Rate (SHR) for one minute. It is 60 percent of your Maximum Heart Rate.

3. Finally, divide your SHR by 4. This will give you your SHR for 15 seconds, or your "target pulse" count. I use this 15-second pulse simply because it is easier to count your pulse for 15 seconds than it is to count it for one full minute.

When you first begin aerobic exercises, you will want to take your pulse count frequently, and to keep it exactly on target if possible. Your Safe Heart Rate represents that number of beats each minute that is safe for your heart, but that will still allow you to gain aerobic training effects. If you stay right on target, you'll know that you are working at a level of exertion that is just right for your body. If you are above target, you will know that you are working too hard and that you will probably experience fatigue. If you are below target, you won't be working hard enough to gain aerobic training effects.

After you have been exercising aerobically for a while you will not have to take your pulse as frequently. Your body awareness will increase, and you will be able to feel when you are working at the right level, when you are working too hard, and when you need to work a bit harder. Until that awareness develops, though, take your pulse frequently and use it as a guide to test your perception of how hard you are working.

If you have been exercising aerobically on a regular basis (at least three times a week for 20 minutes), you may find that exercising at 60 percent of your MHR does not give you an adequate workout. If that is the case, turn to page 20 and compute your heart rate according to the formula given there.

Under nonpregnant circumstances you would find that as you became more aerobically fit, it would take *more* work (jogging longer, walking faster, dancing harder) to bring your pulse count up to target. And, if, for some reason, you became deconditioned through illness or inactivity, it would take *less* work to reach target.

But it's different during pregnancy. You'll still find that deconditioning will have the same result—less work required to bring your pulse rate to target. But you may never, as long as you are pregnant, get to the point where it takes much *more* work to reach target, especially if you started aerobics in your mid- or late-pregnancy. That's because your body is *already* working hard to sustain your pregnancy and to move your extra weight around. This can be discouraging if you insist on gauging the quality of your exercise by how much you do or how fast you do it. So don't let yourself fall into that trap. Judge yourself *only* by your internal measurment of performance—your pulse count. It is a true friend. If you keep your pulse count on target for 20 minutes at least three times each week, you will be getting a good aerobic workout—even if crawling on your hands and knees does it.

My own experience was that right *after* my last two babies were born I was capable of a great deal of aerobic work without tiring. This was especially true after Heather's birth. During my last few weeks of pregnancy with her, I suffered and sweated and swore as I jogged my regular mile and a half. (That was before I knew about pulse-rated exercise.) Two weeks after Heather was born I jogged four miles— feeling as if Mercury had lent me his heel wings. It was won-der-ful! And I've observed the same thing happen with other women who have jogged faithfully (or done some other type of aerobic exercise) regularly during their pregnancies.

But it doesn't *always* work that way. If you're exhausted by lack of adequate sleep, or if you went into labor at midnight after a week-long bout with flu and labored 18 hours, or if you're finding the adjustment to motherhood a particularly difficult one, it may be that you will not be able to work any harder right after your baby is born than you did at the end of pregnancy. Be easy on yourself during these difficult times. Don't fret. Don't overexert. But *do* keep up with your aerobics—it will keep your body fit, your energy level up, and your depressions down. And, of course, monitor your pulse—at first according to the same computations you made during your pregnancy.

After you have been exercising regularly for about four weeks, recompute your Safe Heart Rate. Use the same formula provided earlier in this chapter, but multiply your Safe Heart Rate by .65 instead of .60. Use that target pulse for four more weeks, then multiply by .70, and use *that* target for eight weeks. Then recompute, using .80. Keep exercising faithfully for eight more weeks and—congratulations—you'll be truly aerobically fit. From then on, just keep up the good work. If you do, you'll never again be aerobically unfit.

Helpful Hints

There are a few hints that I'd like to pass on that can make your aerobic exercise safer and more beneficial. Because I'm personally familiar with jogging, walking, and dancing as aerobic exercises, these hints apply only to these forms of aerobics.

1. Get some good shoes.

Walking, jogging, and dancing all involve contact with relatively hard surfaces, and this contact can bother leg joints, feet joints, and lower backs. Your shoes are the only things that come between you and those hard surfaces, so it is important that they provide proper protection, support, cushioning, traction, and flexibility.

It is possible to jog/walk/dance in sneakers. But, generally speaking, sneakers do not provide adequate cushioning, support, or flexibility. They tend to be stiff in the foresoles, and lacking in good arch support and heel cushioning. For this reason, I'd recommend that you purchase a good pair of running shoes.

Buying running shoes can be confusing, through, because there are so many models to choose from. What should you look for? Most experts recommend buying shoes with good protection for the ball of the foot; flexible foresoles; good arch supports; good heel support and cushioning. The shoes must fit you very well, especially from the heel to the ball of the foot, rather than from the heel to the toe. For that reason, it is a good idea to purchase your shoes from a store specializing in running shoes. Salespersons in such stores usually know the special requirements for running.

If you want more information about running shoes, write to Runner's World Magazine, Box 366, Mountain View, California 94042. Each October this magazine publishes a special edition dealing with running shoes, the latest models, and new findings about running feet. You can obtain back issues for a fee.

2. Jog only on a resilient surface.

Grass, a dirt or cinder track, a hardwood floor, all have some "give," which absorbs some of the shock to your joints during jogging. Concrete or asphalt, on the other hand, are much harder on joints. During pregnancy, and up to 10 weeks postpartum (after the baby is born), I think it's especially important to give extra consideration to your joints (remember Relaxin? See chapter 2), and to avoid hard surfaces when jogging.

You can jog in parks, in gymnasiums, or on the local high school or college track. If you have a toddler or two, tracks are a nice solution to the problem of how to jog with children around. Tracks are usually fenced, have large grassy areas in the middle, and, if you're lucky, a sand-filled broad jumping pit. You can jog or walk on the track, while your child(ren) play ball or build sand castles in the broad jumping pit. (Be sure to smooth the sand down when you leave so that the next broad jumper doesn't break an ankle.)

Walking on sidewalks or streets doesn't usually cause joint problems, but pay attention to your body—just in case. If joint problems develop, see your doctor, check your shoes, and then walk on softer surfaces.

3. Maintain proper posture.

Keep your pelvis underneath you, and your body erect but relaxed—whether you walk, jog, or dance. Improper posture is stressful and can lead to strain.

4. Wear appropriate clothing.

Your clothes should be comfortable, nonrestrictive, and should allow you complete freedom of movement.

They should also be appropriate for the weather if you exercise outdoors or in non-air-conditioned/heated rooms.

In warm weather be especially careful to wear cool clothing: shorts and a *cotton* shirt (synthetic blends tend to retain heat). During hot weather our bodies retain heat, and must use a great deal of energy to get rid of the excess heat through perspiration. You'll find that it takes far less work to reach target pulse during hot weather than when it's cooler. And it takes your body at least one week to adjust to hot weather. So go slower when it's hot, and help your body rid itself of that extra heat by dressing in cool clothing.

In cool weather you may want to wear sweat pants and a sweatshirt or light jacket.

In cold weather, add another layer—long johns, maybe, and a warmer jacket. Also, a hat and gloves. You will lose a lot of body heat through an uncovered head, and exposed hands can get frostbitten if it's cold enough. If it's *very* cold, cover your nose, mouth, and chin with something woolen as well.

If the bouncing movement makes your breasts uncomfortable, wear a good supporting bra, one with nonelastic straps and a wide backstrap. If you're naturally big-breasted, you might want underwiring or, as ironic as it sounds, a *padded* bra for extra support.

5. Always warm up before you walk, jog, or dance.

A quick version of the joint warm-ups (#s 1–5), plus some lateral bends and some hamstring stretching will do most of the job. The rest can be done by giving your ankles a little extra work.

6. Always cool down.

I mentioned the reasons for this in chapter 6(# 10). Please try to remember to walk for two or three minutes after you finish your aerobics, and swing your arms as you do it. This will bring your breathing, your heart rate, and your metabolic rate back to nearly normal, and it will help keep blood from pooling in your legs.

If you're jogging, you should do some additional stretching as well, for jogging tends to contribute to shortened lower back and calf muscles and shortened Achilles tendons. These stretches will prevent that from happening.

#15.   Ankle Rolls

1. Stand properly with your feet apart.
2. Put your weight on your left foot.
3. Using your right foot, roll your right ankle until your outside ankle bone is as close to the ground as possible without strain.
4. Hold.
5. Now roll it the other way until your inside ankle bone is as close to the ground as possible without strain.
6. Hold that.
7. Repeat steps 2–5.
0. Then repeat the entire sequence with your left foot.

9. Then use both feet together, and roll both ankles as far to the right as possible.
10. Hold.
11. Then roll as far to the left as possible.
12. Hold that.
13. Repeat steps 9–12.

#16. Back Stretch

1. Stand with your feet apart. Belly tight. Knees relaxed.
2. Gently roll forward until your back is well rounded and your hands are as close to your feet as you can get them without strain.
3. Relax your head, neck, arms, and shoulders.
4. Just hang there for a while.
5. Bend your knees and slowly rise.

#17. Calf Stretch

1. Bend your knees and place your hands on the ground. Belly tight!
2. Walk your feet backward until your toes are on the ground, your heels are off the ground, and your knees are almost straight.
3. Gently lower your heels until you feel a good stretch in both calves. If you don't feel that stretch, walk your feet back even farther. Then try again.
4. Hold.
5. Walk your feet back toward your hands. Bend your knees and rise slowly.

Jogging

I'd like to mention a few things that pertain specifically to jogging.

Many people gallop around for a while, become breathless and exhausted, declare that they've tried jogging and that they hate it. And they never give it a second chance.

But they haven't jogged—they've raced. And that's not the same thing at all.

Jogging is a combination of slow, gentle running (so slow that some people call it slogging) and brisk walking. You'll breathe a bit harder of course, but you should never become breathless, and you should never get ahead of your wind. A good rule of thumb for gauging your rate of speed (besides your pulse count) is this: If you can't carry on a normal conversation (without gasping) as you jog, then you're going too fast and should slow down.

When you first begin jogging you may want to try this combination: run slowly for 1 minute, then walk for 30 seconds, run for 1 minute, walk for 30 seconds, etc. Do that for the entire 20 minutes. If, at any time, your pulse rate goes above target, increase the walking time—walk for, say, 45 seconds or one minute instead of 30 seconds—and slow down your running. If you cannot reach target by following the above combination, increase the *length of time* you run. Don't increase the speed. As you become more and more fit, you will be running more of the time and walking less and less until, at last, you'll be running the entire 20 minutes.

Foot plant, or the way your foot lands on the ground, is also an important consideration. Your toes should always point straight ahead. If you toe out to the sides (a la duck-footed walking) or in to the center (pigeon-toed), you can cause stress in many parts of your legs. If you habitually run on your toes, or if you land toe-first, you can put excessive stress on the muscles in your shins. This can lead to shin splints (muscle separations that *hurt*). If you land heavily on your heel first, it is possible to bruise your heel bone and to develop problems with your Achilles tendons. So try to land on your entire foot and to then roll off your toe. This will spread the impact of contact with the ground over a much larger area, and will not put excessive strain on any one set of muscles or tendons. This may feel strange at first, especially if your calf muscles are tight.

Also, you'll want to keep your shoulders and arms relaxed and your hands loose. You'll probably be more comfortable if you bend your elbows rather than let your arms hang loose. And keep your hands slightly cupped as you would if you were carrying a live canary or an uncooked egg. Don't make tight fists of your hands or you may develop unexplained upper back, neck, or head aches.

And then, breathe regularly and evenly.

That's all there is to it. Now you're on your way. Good (gentle) jogging!

9

How to Create Your Own Exercise Program

*Y*ou can easily create an exercise program that will meet your own individual needs. But before you do, please remember that total fitness can be achieved only by exercising all major muscle groups, as well as your respiratory and circulatory systems. That's not to say that you can't concentrate on your special problem areas. You can. Just don't work those areas to the exclusion of the others.

Chapter 7 includes my suggested Regular Calisthenic Exercise Routine. Look again at that chapter, and try the exercises. If there are some exercises that you don't like or that seem inappropriate for your body, omit them. Then turn to chapter 10, Additional Exercises, and find replacement exercises that work on the same body parts as those exercises you've eliminated. Substitute any exercise(s) that appeals to you.

Chapter 8 deals with walking and jogging, which are aerobic exercises. You can substitue other aerobic exercises: jumping rope, swimming, cycling, aerobic dancing, etc. If you choose to do something besides walking and jogging, fine. But no matter which aerobic exercise you choose, please be certain to monitor your pulse rate in the same way I've suggested in chapter 8.

Sometimes women complain that it is hard to remember which calisthenic exercises to do. And, for sure, it *is* hard to remember a large variety of exercises. It's much easier to remember body parts instead, and to always work from the top of your body down: first in the joint warm-ups, then in the stretches, and finally in the strengthening exercises.

Here's a sample format.

1. *Joint Warm-Ups* (*Don't* neglect these.)

   a. Neck   top
   b. Shoulders
   c. Hips
   d. Knees
   e. Ankles   bottom

2. *Stretches*

   a. Allover (just s-t-r-e-t-c-h-h-h-h)
   b. Lateral abdominals   top
   c. Hamstring
   d. Inner thigh
   e. Calf (if needed)   bottom

55

3. *Strengtheners*

    a. Shoulders   top

    b. Front abdominals

    c. Lower back

    d. Hip/thigh   bottom

4. *Additional exercises for weak or droopy places* (top⟶bottom)

Then add:

5. *Aerobic warm-ups*

6. *Aerobic exercise*

7. *Post-aerobic pullouts*

There, that's all there is to it. You can follow this basic format to start with. As you become more familiar with the exercises and with your own body, you may want to create another type of routine.

10
Additional Exercises

Shoulders and Upper Arms

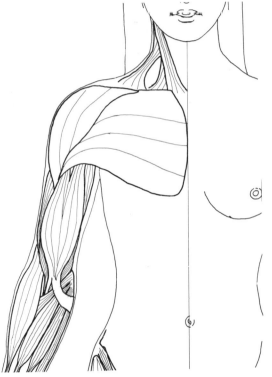

Surface muscles of the shoulder and upper arm—front. *Drawing by Tony Fanning*

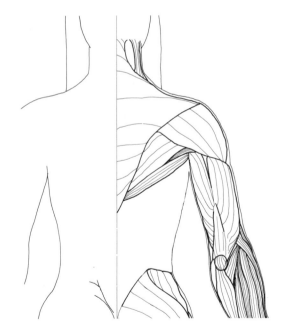

Surface muscles of the shoulder and upper arm—back. *Drawing by Tony Fanning*

It seems to me that one of the problems with women and shoulders is that many of us grew up thinking that it was somehow unfeminine to have strong arms and shoulders. Do you remember hearing things like "Nice girls *don't* do push-ups/chin-ups or hang from trees?" I sure do.

That kind of thinking, of course, can cause problems. For one thing, little girls who believe that never develop the necessary strength to enjoy lots of fun things in childhood. For another, those same little girls frequently grow up into women who want to play tennis or swim or go backpacking. Or they become mothers who must frequently carry their forty-five-pound children. Or they become homemakers responsible for cleaning and painting and pruning trees and building things. Or they become carpenters or farmers. All of these activities require some degree of shoulder/arm strength and/or flexibility. And so it makes no sense that we, as women, should remain programmed against strong, flexible shoulders and arms.

One of the obvious unpleasant side effects of such programming is that we often pay too heavily for doing things that we like to do or that we need to do. How? By having to put up with tight, aching shoulders and arms and necks and heads, or even worse, shoulder injuries. And the price tag on *that* sort of thing can be quite high. Another side effect that is more visible, and, unfortunately, frequently given more importance than the first, is that many women develop soft, flabby upper arms as they grow older (and usually less active).

But take heart. Both side effects can be circumvented by proper exercise. And it is never too late to become strong and fit and flexible. You'll know when you have reached a *minimum* degree of adequate shoulder/arm fitness when you have enough flexibility in your shoulder joints to move your arms easily in all directions without discomfort, and when you can support your own weight when hanging from bars and when doing push-ups.

Pregnancy is as good a time as any other to begin strengthening your arms and shoulders. Maybe even better. Many women complain of postpartum sore shoulders from hanging on to their knees or to the delivery table during the pushing stage of labor. And believe me, a seven-pound baby feels a whole lot heavier when you have to carry it or hold it for a good part of each day. And it doesn't take long before a seven-pound baby weighs eight pounds, and then nine pounds, then ten pounds. Plus, if you plan to carry that baby in a backpack, you are just *asking* for shoulder/neck aches unless you become stronger *first*. So if you begin strengthening your arms and shoulders now, before your baby is born, you will save yourself a lot of discomfort later on.

The exercises I've provided in this section work for both flexibility and strength in the shoulders and arms. They, like all exercises, should be done carefully and slowly at first, just to see how your body reacts to them. If you feel any twinges or pain in your shoulder joints when doing the exercises, you should discuss them in depth with your doctor. Don't worry too much if you hear clicking noises in your shoulders, as long as you feel no pain, twinges, or other discomfort. Clicking of joints often means that you may have some small calcium deposits in the joints. It's nothing to worry about, yet. But you should plan on working regularly and carefully with such joints. Small calcium deposits can become big ones if the affected joints remain inactive. And that can eventually result in tremendously stiff, "frozen" joints. So, please, if you have clicks in your joints, take care of them now.

One last thing. Shoulders and arms and chest and upper back muscles all work together. It is pretty difficult to work with one of these areas without involving the others. This is another good example of how interrelated all parts of you are, and how, by working with one part of you, you are really working with many parts.

#18. Arm Swings

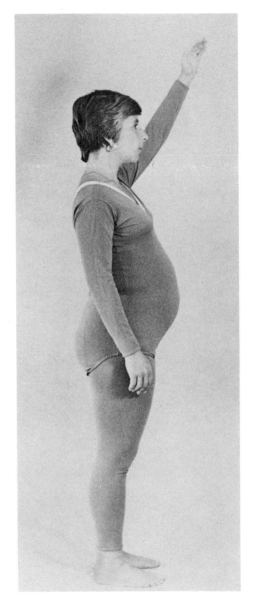 

Cautions and Hints: Don't do this exercise if you are in the middle of a flare-up of arthritis or bursitis of the shoulder joint. For that matter, don't do *any* shoulder exercises then. When the pain subsides you can begin again—slowly. You may want to keep your arm bent at the elbow as you do the exercise, at least until your shoulder muscles become stronger.

Benefits: This involves all the major muscle groups in the shoulders and upper arms. It is primarily designed to give increased shoulder joint flexibility, but it acts as an upper arm firmer as well.

Position: Stand upright in proper posture, feet apart for balance; and arms hanging at your sides.

Procedure

1. Raise one arm—from the shoulder—in front of you. Raise it as high as you can without strain.
2. Then raise it behind you, as high as possible without strain.
3. Repeat that sequence, slowly. The movement should be a fluid one.
4. Change arms and repeat steps 1–3.

More Difficult: Hold a weight bag in each hand. Increase the weight as necessary.

#19. Shoulder Shrugs

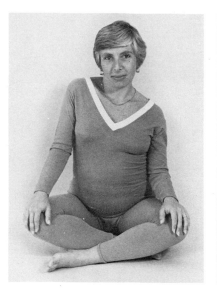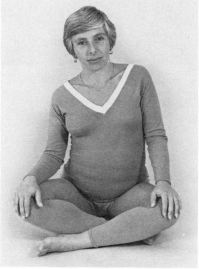

Cautions and Hints: Bad shoulders? Slow and careful, please.

Benefits: This involves shoulder, upper back, and chest muscles. It is great for increasing shoulder flexibility and for relieving upper back tension. (If you carry tension in your neck as well, let your head fall forward as you do this.)

Position: This can be done sitting in tailor position or standing up. Keep your body in proper alignment, belly tight.

Procedure

1. With torso erect and shoulders relaxed, raise your right shoulder as close to your right ear as possible.
2. Relax.
3. Repeat steps 1–2 with your left shoulder.
4. Now, make gentle circles with your right shoulder.
5. Reverse direction and continue the circles.
6. Repeat steps 4–5 with your left shoulder.
7. Now, make circles with both shoulders at the same time.
8. Then "walk" with your shoulders—making half a circle with one shoulder, and then with the other.
9. Reverse directions.
10. For final ultimate challenge: try to write your name, first with your right shoulder, then with your left. You can either print or write in cursive, or, for that matter, type.

   More Difficult: Not needed.

#20. Thumbs Down

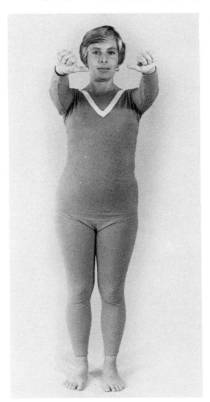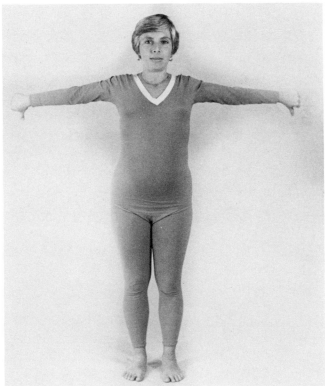

Cautions and Hints: Like all exercises that are good for most shoulders, this can be bad for bad shoulders.

Benefits: This is a great allover shoulder and upper arm exercise. It firms and strengthens both, while adding flexibility to the shoulder joint. It works particularly on those deltoid muscles (which you use when you raise your arm to the side), and is good for people who wish to broaden their shoulders. It also works on the biceps muscles (those in the front of your upper arm that, when you bend your elbow, raise your arm to the front), the triceps muscles (those in the back of your upper arm that raise your arm to the back), and the muscles in the inside of your upper arm (the ones that pull your arms down to your sides).

Position: Stand upright in proper posture, feet apart for balance. Raise both arms straight in front of you to shoulder height. Make loose fists of your hands, but extend your thumbs and point them toward each other. Thumbs should be about 6 inches apart.

Procedure

(Make all twisting motions come from the shoulder joint)

1. Twist both arms until your thumbs point straight down.

2. Then twist your arms the other way until your thumbs point out to the sides as far as they will go.

3. Now, still twisting as described in steps 1–2, slowly open your arms out to the sides as you twist, and bring them as far in back of you as you can. Keep your arms at shoulder level.

4. Still twisting, bring your arms back to starting position.

More Difficult: Do the exercise as described above, but add a gentle bouncing motion to the twist. Begin with your thumbs pointing toward each other. As you twist your arms so that your thumbs point out, draw a big half circle with your hands. And another half circle as you twist again, etc.

#21. Modified Push-Ups

Cautions and Hints: This exercise should be done only after you've mastered Wall Push-Ups (#13). It is important to raise and lower your body in one piece. If you find that your hips sag, go back to Wall Push-Ups. Keep your belly tight.

Benefits: This involves all the shoulder muscles, all the upper arm muscles, the trapezius muscles across the top of your shoulder and neck in back, and the pectoral muscles. It is a great shoulder strengthener, upper arm firmer, and pectoral muscle firmer. (*This* will get you ready for carrying backpacks.)

Position: Rest on your hands and knees, belly tight. Hands should be directly underneath your shoulder line, and wider than shoulder width, with fingers spread. Place your knees directly underneath your hips for starts.

Procedure

1. As you inhale, bend your elbows until you can touch one cheek to the floor. Lower your torso *as a unit*—no sagging.
2. Exhale as you straighten your elbows, raise your torso, and return to starting position.
3. Repeat step 1, touching your other cheek to the mat.
4. Repeat step 2.

More Difficult: In the easy version described above, your hip weight is directly above your knees, and your knees support most of that weight. To make the exercise more difficult, you want your hip weight suspended more between your shoulders and your knees so that your shoulders must do more to support it. So, keep your arms, shoulders, hands, and hips in the same place, and move your knees back. When you have moved them as far as possible (when everything from your knees to your shoulders is straight, and push-ups have become too easy that way), put the balls of your feet on the ground and, keeping your body straight, do push-ups that way. If *that* ever becomes too easy, place your feet on a low bench, and then on a table. (Caution: You must be very, very strong before attempting the last two versions.)

#22.　Forearm Rests

Cautions and Hints: Bad shoulders—careful.

Benefits: This is a good arm and shoulder strengthener. But it's more than that. It's a marvelous abdominal strengthener as well. Anytime you suspend your body weight between your hands (or forearms) and feet, the floor-facing part of you has to work very hard to support that weight. In this case, your entire belly side is working, all the way from your pectorals to your toes.

Position: Rest on your knees and forearms on the floor. Belly tight. Move your knees back until your back is almost flat.

Procedure

1. Place the balls of your feet on the floor. Inhale.
2. As you exhale, raise your knees off the floor until your weight is suspended between your toes and your forearms. Nothing else should touch the floor, and your body should be as straight as possible.
3. Breathe normally, and hold for a slow count of 5.
4. Return to starting position, by putting your knees down. Relax.

More Difficult: Repeat steps 1–2. Then, slowly raise one leg as high as possible without letting your belly sag. (This results in lower back strengthening and fanny firming.) Repeat steps 3–4. Change legs and repeat the entire sequence. Still more difficult? Put your weight bags on your ankles.

ABDOMINALS

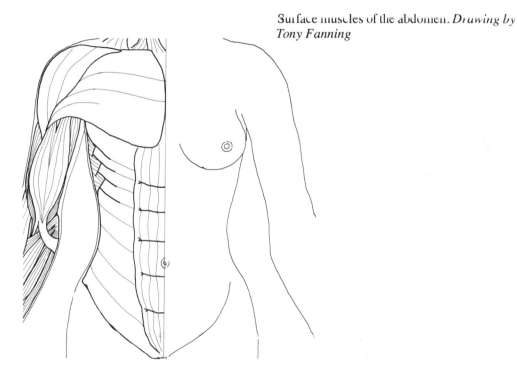

Surface muscles of the abdomen. *Drawing by Tony Fanning*

Many people think of abdominal muscles almost totally in terms of appearance—and our culture is currently down on potbellies and paunchy midriffs. But sleek, strong abdominals are important for more than beauty's sake. Your abdominals help—either directly or indirectly—to support everything from your pelvis up, and are directly involved with your back's state of health.

There are two basic types of abdominal muscles. For brevity's sake, I'll call these "front abdominals" (this term refers to the rectus abdominis muscle) and "lateral abdominals" (the three layers of oblique muscles).

Your front abdominals run right up the center of the front of your belly, from your pelvic bones at the bottom to your ribs on top. They help you bend forward and backward. Front abdominals are the ones that pull your belly in, and are the ones that sag into potbellies when they are loose and flaccid.

The three layers of lateral abdominal muscles wrap around the sides of you.

One layer follows the direction of your ribs; the other two run up and down from your ribs to your pelvis. They meet your front abdominals in the front, and complement your lateral back muscles. Lateral abdominals help you to bend to the sides, and to twist your torso. They hold your belly in and, when firm and strong, define your waistline.

Your lateral abdominals work together with your front abdominals when you cough, sneeze, vomit, breathe heavily, and deliver babies. And strong abdominals help relieve a multitude of problems: difficulty in breathing, constipation, sagging bellies, lower back problems, and poor posture. Strong front abdominals teamed with strong lateral abdominals create an internal muscular girdle that supports your abdominal contents and, when you are pregnant, your baby as well. Abdominals are also important for delivery purposes. If they are strong and capable of hard work, your delivery will be easier, and possibly even shorter, than if they are weak and incapable of helping your uterus expel your baby.

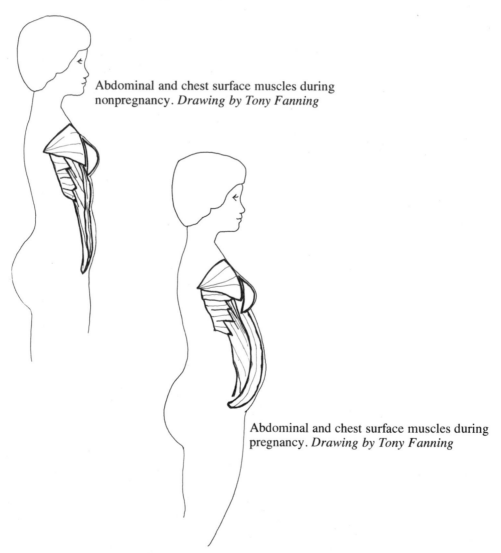

Abdominal and chest surface muscles during nonpregnancy. *Drawing by Tony Fanning*

Abdominal and chest surface muscles during pregnancy. *Drawing by Tony Fanning*

And, even though I've said it before, let me mention once more the importance of strong abdominals in preventing backaches. This is true any time during life, but it is especially true during pregnancy. The increased weight and bulk of your baby, plus the effect of Relaxin in softening joint connective tissue, increases the natural curvature of your lower spine. If your abdominals are strong, they can support the extra weight and bulk, and the back curvature does not pose any real problems. If, on the other hand, they are weak, they cannot support your baby's weight. Your back muscles must help then. And you will probably find yourself standing swaybacked in an attempt to compensate for weak abdominals. That posture not only increases spinal curvature even more, but it is extremely stressful for lower back muscles, and almost always results in nagging backaches.

So, if you begin now to strengthen those abdominal muscles, you'll be much more comfortable during your pregnancy, your delivery will be easier, and you'll probably be pleased with the way your belly looks after your baby is born.

Lest you expect miracles, though, I need to mention one more thing about postpartum bellies. Your belly will *not* snap back into place immediately after delivery like a rubber band that has been stretched and then released. Even if your abdominals are strong and your belly flat, you will have a soft layer of extra tissue on top of your front abdominals. This takes time to reabsorb, but it will disappear—provided that your caloric input does not exceed your energy output, and that you keep exercising your belly muscles. It will take a month or two before you are able to poke your belly and feel strong, hard muscles without that soft stuff on top of them. But don't give up. If you watch what you eat (but please don't diet during pregnancy or while you're nursing without your doctor's approval) and exercise regularly, it *will* happen.

The exercises I've included in this section will help you keep all your abdominals firm and strong, both during pregnancy and afterward too. They are good exercises for everyone, any time in life.

As you do these exercises, you'll feel your abdominals working hard right away. The feeling of work will start at the top of your abdominal area and will work down to your lower belly. So, it's important to hold these exercise positions until you feel your belly working hard all over. And then hold the position as long as possible after that. When your belly begins to quiver or you feel that you really must rest, do so. Relax completely. Then begin again.

You can work harder with your belly muscles than any other muscle group and suffer less afterward. So work hard—these exercises will really firm up your belly.

There are some cautions to keep in mind when working with your abdominals. First, if you have had a heart attack or are a high risk cardiac patient, don't hold the strenuous positions. Instead, do the exercises as instructed, but ignore instructions such as to "hold for a slow count of 10." And, of course, make certain your doctor approves these exercises for you. Second, none of these exercises should be done by people with abdominal hernias.

Occasionally pregnant women develop hernias of the linea alba in their upper abdomen—right beneath the breastbone, between the ribs. This is due to a separation of the two sides or the rectus abdominis muscle, and is usually caused by rib expansion to make space for a growing baby. This type of herniation usually takes care of itself after birth. The other type of hernia is the result of an abnormal slit, or hole, in the muscular abdominal wall. This kind will need surgical repair before you can begin most abdominal exercises.

How do you know if you have a hernia? For one thing, you'll experience pain or discomfort in the herniated area. And frequently there is a soft lump where abdominal contents protrude through the abdominal muscles. And, third, if you press that suspicious area with your fingertips when your belly muscles are tight (for example, in roll-up position [#11]), it will feel very soft. That's because your fingertips will actually push through the muscular wall and you will be feeling the abdominal contents underneath. Naturally, any suspected hernias should be brought to your doctor's attention. And until hernias are repaired, you should avoid most exercises for front abdominal muscles.

No hernias, you say? Great! Study the exercises on the following pages and include them when and where you wish.

#23. Elbow-Knee Roll-Up

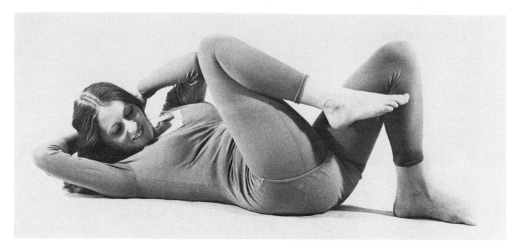

Cautions and Hints: You'll probably notice that none of the abdominal exercises in this book involve sitting up with straight legs. That's because I really believe that bent-legged sit-ups (or roll-ups as I've called them here) are best. In order to sit up with straight legs, it is necessary for your hip flexor and front thigh muscles to work hard. That takes some of the work away from your belly muscles. Not only that, but your lower back muscles must work in a way that can be stressful for weak lower backs, and it is also possible to pull your round ligaments. So, please, do only bent-legged roll-ups (any time in life, not just during pregnancy). And also, please keep everything from your tailbone to your waistline on the floor at all times. teetering on your tailbone can be hard on bad lower backs; if you keep your lower back on the floor, it will be completely supported.

Benefits: Lifting your shoulders and upper body makes the top part of your front abdominals work, while lifting your legs makes the bottom part work. The twisting motion works on your lateral abdominals. This is a good all-abdominal strengthener.

Position: Lie on your back on a carpeted floor. (All abdominal exercises should be done with good padding under your back.) Bend your knees, and place both feet flat on the floor. Clasp you fingers behind your neck.

Procedure

1. Inhale.
2. As you exhale, slowly roll your upper body off the floor. At the same time, raise your bent right leg toward your chest.
3. Twist your upper body, and try to touch your right knee to your left elbow.
4. Hold as you slowly count to 10.
5. Inhale as you slowly return to starting position. Repeat steps 1 and 2, try to touch your left knee to your right elbow. Repeat steps 4 and 5.
6. Exhale as you roll up again, trying to touch your left knee to your right elbow.
7. Hold, breathing normally, as you slowly count to 10.
8. Inhale as you return to starting position.
9. Repeat steps 1–8 until you feel the effort of the work.

#24. Roll Backs

Cautions and Hints: Even though you may feel as if you are *dying* when you do this, rest easy. You can work front abdominals harder than almost any other muscle set and still not ache the next day. All forms of sit-ups are terrible for people with hernias. If you have one, be sure to get it fixed before you try this or any similar exercise.

Benefits: This works primarily on front abdominals and is a great way to declare all-out war on potbellies. You'll be getting some back stretching as well. And, like many of the other exercises that I've included for front abdominals, this should be done regularly for people with bad backs.

Position: Sit on the floor, knees bent and heels about 18 inches from your buttocks. Let your feet touch each other on their inside edges, and spread your knees. Place your hands against the insides of your knees.

Procedure

1. Pull your body into proper alignment.
2. Inhale, tighten your belly muscles.
3. As you exhale, slowly roll your back down until it is touching the floor from you waistline to your tailbone. As your pregnancy increases, you will have less and less bend in your middle, and you may find it necessary to roll down until everything from your tailbone to your shoulder blades touches the floor.

4. Hold as you slowly count to 10. (Or until your belly quivers, whichever comes first.) Breathe!!! And now, poke your belly with your fingers. See how hard you're working!

5. Roll the rest of the way down, until your entire back is resting on the floor.

6. Relax for a minute, then roll to your side, and return to starting position.

   More Difficult: Cross your arms across your chest. When that becomes too easy, clasp your fingers behind your neck. Then, hold your arms straight over your head.

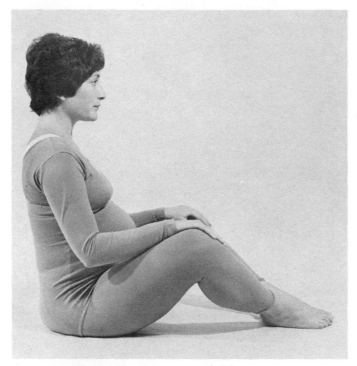

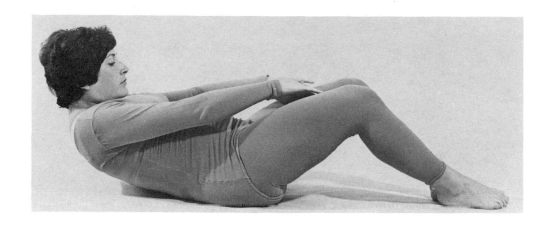

#25. Lowering Legs

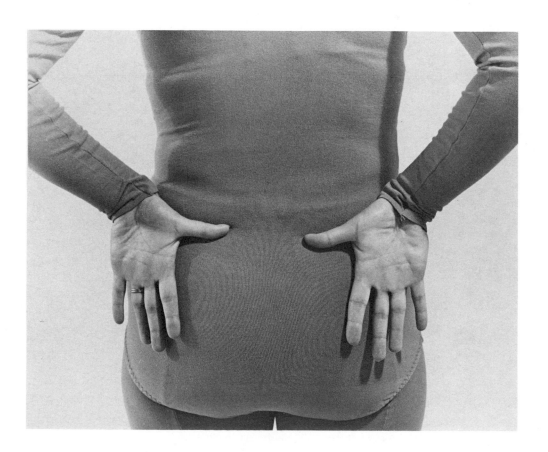

Cautions and Hints: This exercise, improperly done, can be *terrible* for bad lower backs. Please be sure that your back—from your waistline to your tailbone—is always down against your hands and the floor. Sometimes people become overexuberant and lower their legs too far. This causes the pelvis to hyperextend, the lower back to arch off the floor, and all the weight of the legs to then rest on the lower back muscles. At first you may not be able to lower your legs very far. That's okay. As your belly and back become stronger, you'll be able to lower them farther and farther. Please be patient.

Benefits: Strengthens front abdominal muscles, lower back muscles, and the front of the thighs.

Position: Lie on your back on the floor. Bend your knees and place your feet flat on the floor. Tuck your hands underneath your lower back—thumbs snuggled directly beneath the sacroiliac joints on either side of your spine right where the "dimples" are (see illustration), and your fingers spread beneath your buttocks.

Procedure

1. Bring your bent legs as close to your belly possible.
2. Extend them straight up.
3. Now, close your eyes and concentrate on how your lower back feels as it compresses your thumbs, and as your waistline touches the floor. *That* is the feeling you want throughout the exercise. Inhale.
4. As you exhale, keep your left leg straight up, and slowly lower your right leg until it is about halfway between the floor and your left leg.
5. Breathe normally and hold for a slow count of 10.
6. Bend both knees, pull them close to your belly and relax.
7. Repeat steps 2–6, lowering your left leg.

More Difficult: Repeat steps 1–2. Now, carefully, slowly, and with great control, lower *both* legs together. Lower them until you feel your belly working *very* hard, but your back is still pressed against your thumbs and the floor. If you feel your back come up, you know you have gone too far, so raise your legs a bit.

#26. Waist Twists

Cautions and Hints: Again, watch your lower back. Be certain to keep your fanny tucked tightly under at all times. Keep your hips stable, and keep all movement at your waistline and above. This can bother bad knees.

Benefits: This is one way to whittle away that extra waistline flesh. It works on lateral abdominals and back muscles and is good for torso trimming.

Position: Stand upright, with feet apart for balance. Tuck your fanny firmly under and tighten front abdominals and buttocks. Is your posture perfect? Good. Stretch arms out to the sides at shoulder level.

Procedure

1. Inhale.
2. As you exhale, twist your upper body as far to the left as possible without twisting your hips.

3. Breathe normally, and hold as you slowly count to 10.
4. Still keeping front abdominals and buttocks tight and hips stable, slowly return to starting position.
5. Repeat steps 1–4, twisting to the right.

   More Difficult: Clasp your fingers behind your neck.

#27. Side Torso Raises

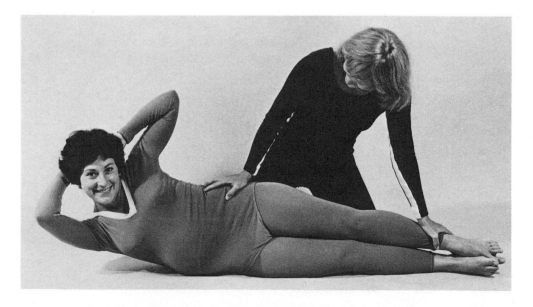

Cautions and Hints: Be sure to stay on your *side*. If you roll back onto your fanny, you'll be working more with front abdominals than with lateral abdominals. Also, round ligaments may holler out.

Benefits: A fine lateral abdominal strengthener and waistline slimmer.

Position: Lie on your side on the floor. Bend your knees, and with both feet on the floor and one foot slightly behind the other, place your feet underneath a low couch or chair. Or, as in the illustration, have someone hold onto your hips and ankles. Clasp your fingers behind your neck, or cross your arms over your chest.

Procedure

1. Inhale.
2. As you exhale, raise your torso straight up to the side, as far as possible. Don't roll onto your fanny.
3. Hold, breathing normally, as you slowly count to 3.
4. Inhale as you slowly return to starting position.
5. Change sides and repeat steps 1–4.

More Difficult: Do it without tucking your feet under something. Or, after you deliver your baby, do it on an incline board.

#28. Leg Overs

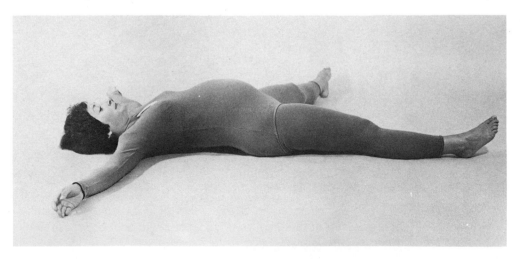

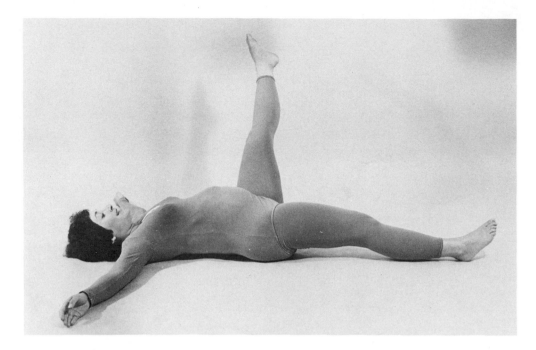

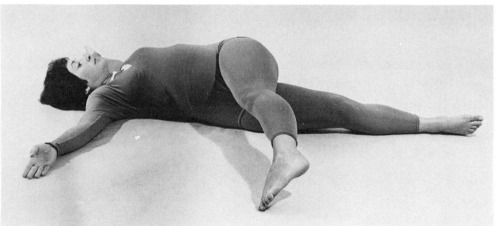

Cautions and Hints: For maximum benefit, keep both shoulders on the floor and your body in a *straight line* at all times.

Benefits: Here you will be getting front abdominal work as you lift your leg, lateral abdominal and back muscle work as you twist, inner thigh stretching and strengthening, and stretching and strengthening of the outer/side thigh as you bring your legs to the sides and raise them off the floor.

Position: Lie on your back on the floor, with your legs straight. Stretch your arms out straight to each side at shoulder level, and make sure your body is in a straight line. Keep your belly tight.

Procedure

1. Breathing normally throughout the exercise, slide your left leg out to the left side as far as possible without lifting your right hip off the floor. (You will ultimately be in semistraddle position, lying down.)
2. Now, slowly raise your left leg until it is straight up.
3. Keep both shoulders on the floor, and slowly lower your left leg until it touches the floor on the *right* side of your body. Your lower body will have to twist in order to do this.
4. Check your body—is it nice and straight? (*Don't* try to touch your right hand with your left foot; it causes your body to collapse and you lose your alignment and stretch.)
5. Slowly raise your left leg again, and slowly bring it back to the straddle position described at the end of step 1.
6. Repeat steps 2–5.
7. Then repeat entire sequence with your right leg.

More Difficult: Tie weight bags on your ankles.

#29. Straddle Stretch

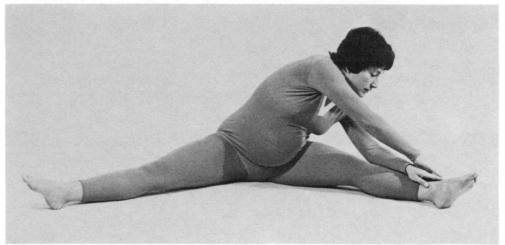

Cautions and Hints: Never make your straddle so wide or lean so far that your knees buckle; you'll lose much of the stretch. Keep your knee caps aimed to the back of you; allowing them to roll in is stressful for knee and hip joints.

Benefits: Stretches and strengthens lateral abdominals and lateral back muscles. Stretches inner thighs, hamstrings, pelvic floor, and lower back muscles too.

Position: Sit in proper alignment with your legs spread in a wide V straddle. If your inner thighs are extremely tight or if you feel teetery sitting this way, make your straddle smaller. Belly tight.

Procedure

1. Stretch your right arm over your head. Inhale.

2. As you exhale, slowly lean to the left as far as possible without raising your right hip off the floor, keeping your shoulders "flat" as if against a wall. Are your knees rolled back? Are they flat against the floor?

3. Hold for a slow count of 5, breathing normally.

4. Keeping your torso as long as possible, slowly raise back to starting position.

5. Repeat steps 1–4 to the other side.

6. Place both hands as close to the left ankle as possible, stretching your torso as long as possible. Knees?

7. Lower your body as far as possible over your left leg.

8. Repeat steps 3–4.

9. Change sides and repeat steps 6–8.

10. Now, wrap your right hand around the *outside* of your left ankle (the side pointing behind you).

11. Repeat step 7. Repeat steps 3–4.

12. Change sides, and repeat steps 10–11.

Backs

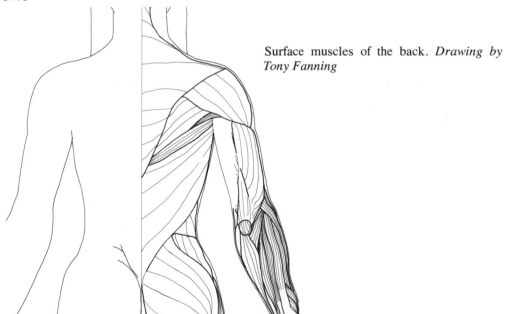

Surface muscles of the back. *Drawing by Tony Fanning*

Not long ago, one of the women in my class related a tale that I've heard much too often. Her lower back had been aching for several weeks. In her sixth month of pregnancy, concerned and uncomfortable, she brought this to her doctor's attention. His response was to tell her, first, to hold her belly in, and, second, that backaches were common during pregnancy. He also added that she might as well get used to that backache, because it might just hang around until she delivered her baby.

But, the lady has spunk, and instead of giving up, she tried something else instead. She stopped wearing high-heeled shoes, and started strengthening and stretching her lower back and strengthening her belly. Two weeks after that her backaches were no longer a problem.

Now, I don't mean to imply that all backaches can be relieved by proper footwear and exercise. There are many causes of back problems: vertebral, disk, nerve, muscle, or ligament abnormalities; abnormalities in other body parts (such as kidneys, bladder, etc.). So it is very important to have your doctor properly diagnose the cause of any back pain you might be experiencing.

But, after medical examination, you'll *probably* find that your backache is the result of weak belly and back muscles. The fact is that there is a shockingly high percentage of back problems and the flabby bellies and weak and/or tight back muscles that usually accompany them. We simply don't have to use our bodies as much in everyday life as people did before all the laborsaving devices were introduced. And so our bodies have become weak and saggy. During pregnancy, this weakness and sagginess is complicated by Relaxin, increased weight and bulk, and increased lower back curvature. It's not surprising that so many pregnant women have trouble with their backs, but the truth is that most of these troubles are unnecessary. Exercise, proper footwear, and good carriage make up the best prescription possible for most backaches. It certainly beats taking pills that leave you feeling half alive and that may have harmful effects on your baby, or having to stay in bed most of the time, or just having to put up with a nagging backache.

So exercise is usually good for relieving backaches. But there is another problem here. There are many things you *shouldn't* do until your back becomes stronger. If you lift a heavy object (including your own body weight) improperly, or twist your back in an awkward position, or bend in a way that causes stress on the muscles or pressure on the nerves, your weak back muscles might go into spasm. And muscle spasm is what you feel when your back really hurts.

To prevent this possibility, I'd like to give you some hints on what *not* to do for your aching back.

Standing

Chapter 3 is devoted to proper posture. I can't even begin to tell you how important proper posture is in preventing back pain—any time in life. It's so fundamental that poor posture almost guarantees back problems.

Don't stand with your weight on one leg and your opposite hip jutting out. This throws your pelvis out of alignment, and frequently results in back strain, or sciatic nerve pain.

Don't stand like that and hold your baby on your high hip.

Don't stand with your knees locked, your back swayed, and your front abdominals loose. Many pregnant women stand this way in an attempt to compensate for the extra weight and bulk they're carrying. It's murder on your back. (Chapter 3 will tell you why.)

Do stand in proper posture: weight evenly distributed on both feet, feet slightly apart, knees straight but loose, belly tight, fanny tucked under, and back straight. This posture will provide support for your lower back, and will pull your spine into good alignment.

Sitting

Don't slump and allow your weight to rest on your lower back, with your shoulders rounded and your belly loose. This puts the weight of your baby and all your abdominal contents on unsupported lower back muscles.

Do sit on your sitting bones and pull your back up straight from there. This pulls your pelvis and your spine into perfect alignment. Your lower back will feel no strain, but your upper back muscles—the ones between your shoulder blades—may find this hard work if they are used to slumping.

Sleeping or Resting

Don't sleep on your back with your legs out straight. This will cause your lower back to arch slightly so that it is not supported by the mattress.

Do sleep on your back with a pillow or two under your knees. This will round your back so that it will be completely supported.

Don't sleep on your stomach with your legs out straight. This also causes your back to arch.

Do sleep on one side. Bend the opposite knee and bring it up close to your belly. This will round your lower back and eliminate strain.

Do sleep on your side with your knees bent close to your belly. In this position your back is rounded and supported. Sometimes it helps while sleeping on your side to put a pillow between your knees so that the weight of your top leg does not rest on the lower back muscles on that side. When I was pregnant, it helped to put a small pillow under my belly, one behind my back, and one under my head.

Lifting Heavy Objects

This includes small children, sacks of groceries, etc.

Don't bend over from your hips, grasp an object that is low, and try to lift it by straightening your back. Lower back muscles do most of the lifting this way.

Do place one foot slightly ahead of the other. Keep your feet apart, and pointing out rather than straight ahead. Squat down with your knees wide. Pull the object close to your torso, tuck your fanny under, and lift by straightening your legs. Here thigh and belly muscles do the lifting.

Do squat down, as described above, and pull the object close to your body. Raise your fanny until your legs are halfway straightened. Then grip with your thigh muscles, and raise your torso. (If you let your legs become straight or lock your knees, your lower back muscles, once again, become the lifters. So keep your knees bent.)

Don't reach over your head to bring a heavy object down from a high place. This will make you bend backward with your back swayed.

Do climb up on a ladder or stool until the object is approximately opposite your mid-torso. Tuck your fanny under, keep your back straight, and using your arm and shoulder muscles, pull the object close to your body. Climb down from there. (Or better yet, get someone else to fetch that object.)

Putting Heavy Objects Down

Don't bend over from your waist and try to set an object on the floor. Your lower back muscles must bear the brunt of the object's weight.

Do squat down, as described above, with the object close to your body. Use your arm and shoulder muscles to put the object down.

Don't try to place a heavy object on a high shelf by struggling to get it over your head. This, once more, will cause your back to bend backward, and become swayed.

Do clutch the object close to your torso, climb a ladder or stool until your belly is about even with the shelf. Keep your abdominals tight, your fanny tucked under, and your back straight. Then use your arm and shoulder muscles to put the object on the shelf.

Carrying Heavy Objects

Don't rest the object on your belly to compensate for its weight. This will make you bend backward and your back will sway.

Don't rest the object on one hip (this includes children). This will make the hip jut out and will throw your pelvis out of alignment.

Do keep your back straight, your fanny tucked under, your belly tight. Carry the weight with your arms and forearms.

Pushing and Pulling Vacuum Cleaners

. . . and hoes, and rakes, and mops, and shovels, and other such things.

Don't keep your feet together and bend from your waist as you push/pull the vacuum cleaner. Lower back muscles do a lot of the work this way.

Do place one foot slightly ahead of the other. Keep your feet well apart, your tummy tight, fanny tucked under, and back straight. Push/pull with your arm/ shoulder muscles, not with your back.

Don't make the pushing/pulling motion from, say, your right side to straight in front of you and back again. Your lower back muscles will have to work too hard.

Do stand properly and push and pull by starting at your right side. But then move the vacuum *diagonally* across the front of your body, from right to left and back again. This puts most of the work in your arms and shoulders.

Don't ever use a shovel by bending from your waist.

Do place your feet apart and bend your legs with each thrust of the shovel.

Working in the Kitchen

Don't attempt to compensate for too-low counter tops by hunching over them. Backs become tired this way.

Don't attempt to compensate for too-high counters by leaning backward.

Do stand with your feet apart, fanny tucked under, belly tight, and back straight. Compensate for inadequate counter height by raising or lowering your arms.

Do get a stool that will allow you to sit down at a perfect height.

Bathing Wiggly Children

Don't hunch over the bathtub with rounded back.

Do squat down, as described above. Or better yet . . .

Do strip down and climb into the tub while you bathe that delicious little body.

Don't, if your child is still small enough to bathe in a plastic tub, place that tub on anything so low that it makes you bend over to reach the baby.

Do place the tub on a kitchen counter, a changing table, or anything else that will allow you to stand upright with your back straight as you bathe the baby. The same goes for changing diapers, etc.

Exercises

Some of the exercises I've seen prescribed for weak backs can actually make back problems worse. So, whenever you do back exercises, keep a careful inward eye wide open. If your back ever feels twinges or pain, you can be pretty certain that that exercise is not for you right now.

The following types of exercises can cause problems. Try to understand the basic movement in each type and then watch out for any exercises that incorporate that basic movement.

Don't do any of the following types of exercises unless your abdominals and back muscles are *very* strong, and even then be suspicious of them.

1. Leg Raises where, lying on your back with your legs straight, you lift both legs off the floor at the same time. This makes your lower back arch and puts most of your leg weight on your lower back muscles. Weak lower backs simply can't take that. These exercises are usually prescribed for strengthening abdominals. Avoid them like the plague—there are safer ways to strengthen your belly.

2. Leg Lowers. These are first cousins to leg raises, and are terrible for weak backs for all the same reasons. Here, instead of raising your legs up from the floor, you lower them both all the way to the floor. I've included one modified version of this type of exercise (#25) which I think is all right, but read the cautions carefully before you do it.

3. Straight-Legged Sit-Ups. You'll find these recommended in lots of exercise books. But that doesn't make them good. Straight-legged sit-ups should never be done by people with bad backs because the lower back muscles must work too hard. Besides that, thigh and hip flexor muscles must work hard too. That's fine for thighs and hip flexors, but it cheats the front abdominals out of a lot of work. For maximum belly benefit, as well as back support, do bent-legged sit-ups instead. And while you're pregnant, always leave your back on the floor from your waistline to your tailbone. Your back will be supported this way, and your belly will work hard.

4. Rocking Horse. This is almost impossible to do when you're more than a couple of months pregnant. But I'm going to throw it in just in case you are ever tempted to try it. Here you lie on your stomach and lift both legs, both arms, and your head at the same time. That puts all the weight of all those appendages on your back muscles. (People who should *know* better might tell you this is just fine. Don't believe them. If you ever try it, lift just *one* arm or leg at a time. When you're *very* strong it's okay to try (carefully at first) lifting everything all at once.)

The next group of exercises can actually help strengthen backs. They are good exercises. But if your back is extremely weak or if you feel any discomfort when doing these types, you'd be smart to table them until your back is stronger.

1. Lateral Bends. These exercises involve standing or kneeling and then leaning first to one side and then the other. You can minimize stress by keeping your fanny tight and tucked under and by leaning from your waistline and above. Don't let your hips jut out.

2. Torso Churns. Here, you stand or kneel and make big circles with your upper body.

3. Back Arches. Any exercise in which your back must arch is potentially stressful for your weak lower back. Stress is minimized if you do these while lying down on your back or kneeling. *Always* keep your belly tight.

4. Toe Touches. I talked some about locked knees in chapter 3, Proper Posture Is Important, but just in case you've forgotten, I'll repeat that message. Locked knees can contribute to back problems and knee problems. If you touch your toes from a standing position, be certain to keep your knees relaxed, but straight—never lock them. Also, when you rise from that position, bend your knees. That will make your front abdominals do the lifting instead of your lower back.

Footwear

Don't wear high-heeled shoes. They often make you lean backward, and are terrible for people with bad backs.

Do wear low- or flat-heeled shoes that are healthy for your feet—even if they look like gunboats. They will help keep your pelvis in proper alignment, and will do a lot to prevent backaches.

Do walk with bare feet whenever possible. This will wake up the muscles in your feet and will help them stay strong and healthy.

And, now on to what you *should* do for your weak back. The exercises in this section are ones that I've used in my prenatal fitness classes for the past four years, and I've found them both safe and effective. As always, though, go carefully at first. See how *your* back is going to react to them.

#30. Angry Cat

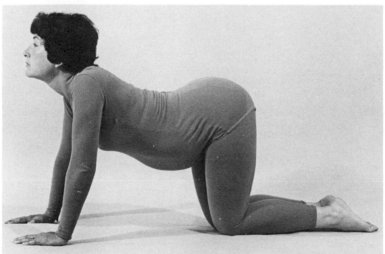

Cautions and Hints: Whenever you are on your hands and knees, it is very important to keep your belly muscles tight. If you let them sag, your back will sway, and your lower back muscles will be supporting much unnecessary weight—and that can lead to strain. If, even with that precaution, you feel any stress in your lower back while doing this exercise, do Pelvic Tilts (#10) instead. When doing this exercise, pretend that you have two red buttons glued to your body, one right between your shoulder blades in back and one right between your bottom two ribs in front.

Benefits: This is a great exercise for strengthening, as well as increasing flexibility in, lower backs. It also strengthens and firms front abdominals, buttocks and upper/back thigh muscles. It stretches front abdominals and upper back muscles.

Position: Kneel on all fours. Keep your belly tight, your arms straight (don't lock elbows), and try to make your back absolutely flat.

Procedure

1. Tighten your buttocks, and your belly even harder. Inhale.

2. As you exhale, tuck your chin against your throat, and, tucking your fanny under even harder, push up with your shoulder blades. Get that red button as close to the ceiling as possible.

3. Breathing normally, tighten your chin and fanny even harder, and pull your hips even further forward. Push up harder with your shoulder blades. (By this time this position should feel like work.)

4. Hold, breathing normally, for a slow count of 5.

5. *Slowly* return to starting position—don't just collapse.

6. Retighten belly—hard. Lift your chin, push your fanny out. Inhale.

7. As you exhale, push the red button between your ribs as close to the floor as possible. You should feel your front abdominals stretch.

8. Hold for a slow count of 5, breathing normally.

9. Slowly return to starting position.

More Difficult: Do Back Tuck and Arch (#31).

#31. Back Tuck and Arch

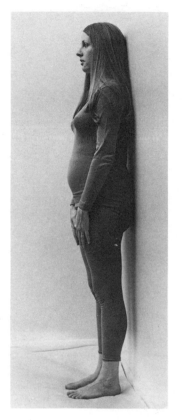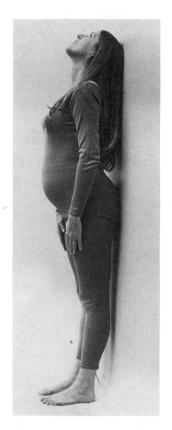

Cautions and Hints: Like all back strengthening exercises, this should be done cautiously at first, to see how your back reacts to it. If the second part, the arching part, bothers you, go back to #30, Angry Cat. Make this movement a controlled, fluid one.

Benefits: This strengthens lower back, buttocks, back/thigh, and abdominal muscles. It stretches back and belly muscles. If you need to bend your legs to flatten your back to the wall, you'll be working the muscles in the front of your thighs too.

Position: Stand with your back against a wall, feet apart. Move your heels out 2 inches from the base of the wall. Place your fanny, your shoulder blades, and the base of your skull against the wall. Let your arms hang comfortably at your sides.

Procedure

1. Inhale.
2. As you exhale, tighten your belly and buttocks, tuck your fanny under, and press your waistline against the wall.

3. Place your fingers between your waistline and the wall. If there is more than one fingers width between them, bend your knees until you feel your waistline press flat against the wall.

4. Hold, breathing normally, as you slowly count to 5.

5. Slowly return to starting position.

6. Then, belly very tight, place the panty line part of your fanny against the wall. Inhale.

7. As you exhale, arch your back. Keep your skull against the wall, but allow everything else between your fanny and your head to come away from the wall. Is your belly still tight?

8. Breathe normally and hold for a slow count of 5.

9. Slowly return to starting position.

   More Difficult: Not necessary.

#32. Wall Walk

Cautions and Hints: This *must* be done slowly and with great control. Pretend that once any part of your back touches the wall, it becomes stuck—you can move it as long as it is *on* the wall, but it can't be pulled *away* from the wall.

Benefits: This increases spinal flexibility and strengthens spinal muscles. You are also working with the front abdominal and lateral abdominal and back muscles, and front thigh muscles. It looks pretty easy—just wait!

Position: Stand with your back to a wall. Move your feet so that your heels are about 18 inches from the wall. Bend your knees and let your upper body collapse over your legs. Keep your belly tight.

Procedure

1. Slowly begin at the base of your spine and, touching one vertebra to the wall at a time, raise your upper body until your back is flat against the wall from your tailbone to your shoulder blades. (You're stuck, remember.) Place your head against the wall too.

2. Now, with your back against the wall at all times, s-l-o-w-l-y lean as far to the left as you can without coming unstuck anyplace. Breathe!

3. S-l-o-w-l-y return to your upright position.

4. Repeat steps 2–3, leaning to the right.

More Difficult: Not necessary.

#33. Iliopsoas Muscle Stretch and Strengthener

Cautions and Hints: The iliopsoas muscles attach to your spine in your lower back and then run diagonally across your pelvis and attach to your thigh bone. If psoas muscles are too loose or too tight, they can cause many back problems, including shortening so much that one hip is higher than the other. If you have a really tight lower back, do this exercise daily.

Benefits: Stretches and strengthens iliopsoas muscles. Also, you'll be getting some inner thigh and pelvic floor stretching.

Position: Lie on your back on the floor, with your knees bent and feet flat on the floor. Place your feet together and rest your arms at your sides.

Procedure

1. Allow your right knee to fall to your right side.
2. Hold for a count of 5.
3. Return your right leg to starting position. Repeat several times.

4. Repeat steps 1–3 with your left knee.

5. Now, place your right hand on top of your right knee.

6. Make circles with your right knee—as large as your arm will allow you to make. Go first in one direction and then in the other.

7. Repeat steps 5–6 with your left knee.

More Difficult: Not necessary.

#34. Lower Back Stretch

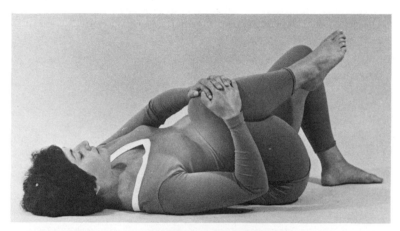

Cautions and Hints: This is a wonderfully relaxing exercise to do for your achy, tight lower back. But it *is* one of those exercises that becomes less easy as you become more bulgy. It helps if, then, you bring your knees around the *sides* of your belly instead of close to the center of your belly.

Benefits: Stretches lower back and hip flexor muscles. Contributes to increased lower back and pelvic flexibility.

Position: Lie on your back. Bend your knees and place your feet flat on the floor.

Procedure

1. Clasp your fingers around your right knee.
2. Gently pull your knee as close to your chest as possible. Relax your lower back and try to let your fanny roll off the floor as you pull.
3. Hold for a slow count of 3.
4. Release.
5. Repeat steps 2–4 several times.
6. Now, grasp your left knee and repeat steps 2–5.
7. Finally, grasp both knees with your hands (right hand on right knee, left hand on left knee), and pull both knees close to your chest (or outside your belly).
8. Repeat steps 2–5.

More Difficult: Not necessary.

Hips and Thighs

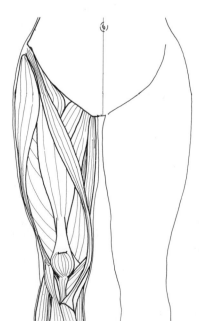

Surface muscles of the hip and thigh—front.
Drawing by Tony Fanning

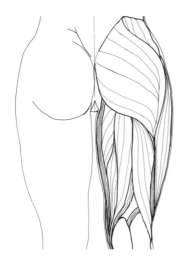

Surface muscles of the hip and thigh—back.
Drawing by Tony Fanning

Probably 90 percent of the women in my classes worry about their hips and thighs. Although some moan about leggy leanness most feel that their hips and thighs are too big or too flabby, or, worse, *both* too big and too flabby. "Cottage cheese thighs," they mutter and smack their legs. Or "lard ass." Or "flabby buns." And, it is true that many women carry extra weight right *there*.

Even though we would all like to believe in athletic good fairies with magic wands who do away with our flabby flesh, deep down inside, we all know the answer to our problem. And under normal, mortal circumstances, the answer is simple. We have wobbly fannies and thighs because *we don't move our legs enough.*

Think about it. How often do you kick, or run, or skip, or hop, or jump, or squat, or raise your legs high, or swim, or climb stairs, or jog, or bike, or walk distances, or dance? Not very often? Well, as much as I hate to say it, *that* is a big part of the reason you don't like the way your hips and thighs look. You are simply not moving enough.

Hips and thighs go together. When you work with one area you almost always work with the other area. And the best way to work with them both is to move your legs (and your body)—lots.

Pregnancy can be a discouraging time for women beset with hip/thigh worries, because most pregnant women put on extra inches in their hip/thigh area. Some of this extra girth is due to the effect of Relaxin and pelvic spread. Some of it, thanks to Mother Nature's foresight, is just good, normal, healthy fat that our bodies accumulate during pregnancy to feed that baby in case of famine or other such natural disasters. This kind of extra spread will probably take care of itself after the baby is born.

But, if in your heart of hearts you know that your prenatal food cravings lean toward banana splits, or that your entire exercise program consists of a daily bout with the vacuum cleaner, then you have something to worry about. Extra weight caused by extra calories will stay there unless you start eating less; and extra inches due to lack of proper exercise won't go away after you deliver your baby.

The calisthenics I'm including here will help you get started in your fight against fanny spread and flabby thighs. The bad news is that your thigh and buttocks muscles will probably ache when you first start these exercises. That's because you must use those muscles all the time—when you walk, when you get up and down from the floor, etc. If you keep working, the soreness will become less and less. If your knees hurt, though, that's something else. That means you need to make your knees stronger before you continue the exercises. The good news is that thigh and buttocks muscles are some of the easiest muscle groups to firm up—the muscles are long and large, and they can become very firm in a relatively short time with proper exercise. The exercises won't get rid of extra weight in your hips and thighs, though. Only cutting down on your caloric intake will do that. But, before you attempt to diet during pregnancy or while you're nursing, you'd best check with your doctor.

And, if your hips and thighs are one of your problem areas, don't forget your aerobic exercises. There's practically nothing as good for firming up hips and thighs as a regular aerobics program.

#35. Leg Extensions

I am going to go into a lot of detail with this exercise because I think that it will help you understand more about how you are put together in your hip/thigh area, and because it illustrates many of the principles behind hip/thigh flabbiness and/or firmness.

Cautions and Hints: Theoretically, this could be a problem for people with bad hips. If it bothers you, stick to Side Leg Lifts (#38) until your hip joints are in better condition.

Position: Stand erect in proper posture, with your belly tight, your fanny tucked

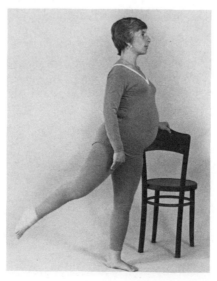

under, and your back straight. Place your feet apart, with your weight evenly distributed. Hold onto a dresser, a table, or the back of a chair with one hand. You will be using that dresser, etc. for balance, so don't lean on it. Don't lock your knees.

Procedure

1. Extend one leg out in back of you. Keep your back straight—don't lean forward.
2. Now, put your hand on your fanny. Feel how tight it is? Touch the back of your thigh. Tight too, right? Now touch your lower back. Same thing: taut muscles. That's because every time you extend your leg in *back* of you, you are making all of your backside muscles work.
3. With your leg still in back of you: raise it and lower it gently; make circles with it; move it from side to side. As you are moving your leg, use your free hand to feel your hips, thighs, and lower back. What's happening now?
4. Just to compare actively working muscles with passive muscles, lower that leg and stand on both feet. Your muscles are now working passively instead of actively. Feel your fanny, thighs, lower back. Feel the difference? Good.

5. But maybe you are more concerned about the side of your thighs—right where the saddlebags are. Okay. Pull your body into alignment and extend that same leg out to the side, ankle bone facing the ceiling.
6. Touch the side of your thigh, the side of your hip, and the back of your thigh and hip. Now which is working hardest? The side, of course.
7. Try turning your foot so that the top of it faces the ceiling. Touch your thigh all over. Now where are you working hardest? Now it's the top of your thigh.

8. Just as you did before, keep that side extension, and move your leg all around. Raise it. Lower it. Make circles with it. Swing it. Does the movement make any difference? How?

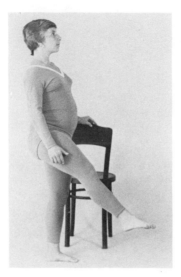

9. Now, still standing properly, extend your leg out in front of you. (Don't worry about height; you're just trying to learn about your body, not audition for the American Ballet Theatre.)

10. Touch your leg all over and determine which muscle groups are working hardest now. Touch your hips. The leg you're standing on. That big, strong muscle you feel on the top of your thigh is the rectus femoris. Just by raising your leg in front of you, you are strengthening that muscle, as well as others.

11. Change the position of your foot, and as you do it, feel your thigh. Figure out how the workload changes when you turn your toes in, when you turn them out.

12. Does moving your leg make a difference? It does. The higher it goes, the harder it must work. And whenever you *hold* a position, muscles work harder than they do when you slide in and out of that position.

What I hope you see by now is that your thigh muscles and your hip muscles are all interrelated and interdependent, and that by working with your legs you are, in fact, working with your hips as well. I also hope that you see that by putting your leg in back of you, you work with all your backside muscles; that by extending it to the side, you work with the muscles on the sides of your thighs; and that by raising it in front of you, you work with all the muscles on the front of the leg you're raising. You also work with the muscles of your standing leg, which must remain firm and tight to keep you upright. Because leg extensions require thigh/hip muscles to support the weight of your extended leg, they are a good way to firm up your hips and thighs.

The above is an oversimplification of the subject of hips and thighs and the work they do, but I hope it gives you some idea of what is going on in your hips and thighs. And leg extensions *are* wonderful for creating firm hips and thighs. In fact, if you never did much else, 15 minutes worth of leg extensions each day would give you wonderful hips and thighs.

Of course, leg extensions are not the only way to strengthen and firm hips and thighs. There are lots of other ways too. I really prefer some of the other ways— jogging, walking, swimming, skipping, jumping, squatting, biking—because they involve total body movement, and so much the better for your total body.

Many exercises that are great for hips and thighs, though, require caution on the part of people with bad knees. So, go slowly, carefully, and see how your knees react. If you already know that your knees are weak, do Knee Lifts (#44) and Knee Pushes (#43) to strengthen those weak places.

#37.   String of Beads

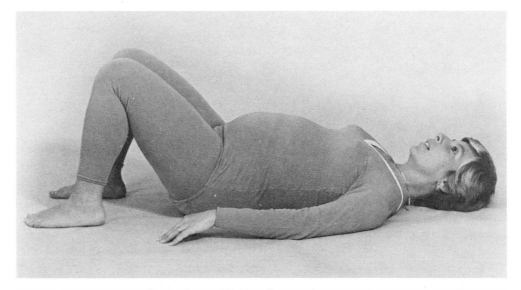

Cautions: This movement should be a *controlled* one, so go slowly and very carefully. *Never* allow your weight to rest on your neck. Keep it resting on your shoulders, arms, and feet instead.

This might be difficult for some people to do, especially if you have any fused joints, scoliosis, or a really tight, inflexible back. If you find that your back simply refuses to cooperate, just keep going as long as you feel no pain. Go slowly and carefully. It takes time, but with practice your back *can* become more flexible. Be sure to do this on a *carpeted* floor.

Benefits: I learned this exercise in a modern dance class, and I've never given it up because it does such beautiful things for hips and thighs. It involves almost all your gluteal muscles, and the back/side/inner front thigh muscles as well. Not only that, but it is a super back exercise. The rolling motion not only contributes to spinal flexibility, but done correctly, this exercise can help realign your spine if it has fallen into slouchy misalignment. Remember, go slowly. This should make you feel as though you are really working.

Position: Lie on your back on the floor. Bend your knees. Put your feet on the floor, and at least 18 inches apart. Let your arms relax next to your sides, palms down.

Procedure

1. Tighten your abdomen and your buttocks.

2. As you exhale, press your waistline to the floor and lift your tailbone off the floor. (This is just the Pelvic Tilt, #10.)

3. Now, breathing normally and keeping your belly and fanny really tight, slowly lift your hips by rolling your backbone off the floor *one vertebra at a time,* just as you would lift a string of beads by holding one end of the string and lifting one bead at a time. Keep rolling until your hips are very high and your weight is resting on your shoulders, arms, and feet.

4. Hold for a count of 5. (Feel how hard the muscles in your fanny are; the muscles in the back of your thighs?) Now, slowly r-o-l-l back down to starting position, one vertebra at a time.

More Difficult: Not needed.

#37. Side Leg Lifts

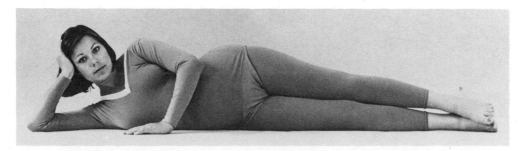

Cautions and Hints: Build up slowly and gradually if your hips are bad. Do just one set at first, and then add one set at a time.

Benefits: This is a good exercise for loosening up stiff hip joints before they "freeze." It's also good for evening up uneven hips, provided the unevenness is muscular in origin. It also firms hips and thighs because it uses the gluteal muscles, the side thigh muscles. It stretches inner thighs and pelvic floor.

Position: Lie on your right side on the floor. Place your knees, hips, and shoulders in a straight line. Place your left hand on the floor in front of your ribs, and support your head with your right hand. Keep your belly tight.

Procedure

1. Keep your left outside ankle bone up and your left leg straight but not stiff, slowly (count slowly to 5) raise it as high as you can without bending your knees or changing the position of your body.

2. Hold for a slow count of 5, breathing normally.

3. Lower to starting position as you slowly count to 5.

4. Repeat steps 1–3 with right leg.

More Difficult: Put weight bags on your ankles.

#38. Partial Side Leg Lifts

Cautions and Hints: Those with bad hips go slowly.

Benefits: This firms the side/back of the thighs (saddlebag area) and buttocks.

Position: Lie on your right side on the floor. Place your body in a straight line. Support your head with your right hand. Place your left hand on the floor in front of your ribs. Keeping your left leg straight, twist it until your heel faces the ceiling and your toes face the floor. Keep that foot alignment, and place the ball of your foot firmly on the floor. Belly tight?

Procedure

1. Slowly count to 5 as you raise your left leg as high as you can without bending your knees, changing the position of your body, or losing your foot alignment.
2. Hold as you slowly count to 5.
3. Count to 5 as you slowly lower your leg.
4. Repeat steps 1–3 with the other leg.

More Difficult: Put weight bags on your ankles.

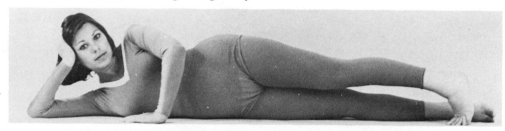

#39. Inner Thigh Lifts

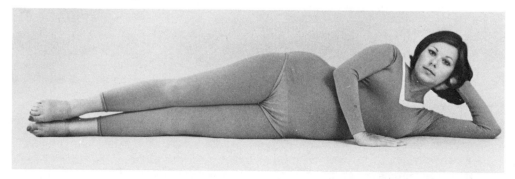

Cautions: It's tempting here to roll back onto your fanny. Don't. Stay on your side.

Benefits: This firms and strengthens the inner thigh muscles on the bottom leg and stretches the outside hip and thigh muscles on the bottom side. It firms the hip and lateral abdominals on the top side.

Position: Lie on your left side on the floor. Support your head with your left hand, and place your right hand on the floor in front of your ribs. Keep your body in a straight line, with your belly tight.

Procedure

1. Slowly count to 3 as you raise both legs together, as high as they will go without rolling onto your buttocks. (You won't get much height here.)
2. Hold for a slow count of 5.
3. Slowly lower your legs as you count to 3.
4. Change sides, and repeat steps 1–3.

More Difficult: Wear heavy shoes or weight bags.

#40. Hip Roll

Cautions: During this exercise, you will be putting a lot of stress on your shoulder joints. Go slowly and carefully, and if you feel any pain in your shoulder joints that means . . . right! Back to shoulder strengtheners for you! Wrists hurt? Strengthen *them*. Knees bothering you when you do this? Try going slowly and not twisting your body quite so far. If, after that modification, they still hurt, back to knee strengtheners. If round ligaments are a problem, simply go less vigorously.

Muscles: This exercise works on your gluteals, your thigh muscles (especially the back ones), and those lateral abdominal muscles that pull in your waistline. Not only that, but shoulder muscles, arm muscles, and middle and upper back muscles are working. This is a *good* allover exercise.

If, in your last trimester, this becomes too strenuous, you should substitute other exercises instead.

Position: Sit on the floor and lean back on your arms. Put your legs out in front of you, and straighten them out as much as you can without lifting your toes off the floor. Your knees will be slightly bent.

Procedure

1. Keeping your stomach tight, lift your hips off the floor.
2. Twist your body so that one hip faces the floor and the other hip faces the ceiling.
3. Touch the floor-facing hip to the floor.
4. Lift, twist, and touch the other hip to the floor.

More Difficult: Rest one leg on top of the other leg. Repeat the exercise as above.

#41. Kneeling Walk

Cautions: This is one of those exercises that can be terrible for people with bad knees. If you are a member of the Bad Knees Club, please strengthen those knees before you do this. At first, you will probably feel awkward and ungraceful. It requires good balance and strong rectus femoris muscles. But don't give up—keep trying. If you are weak, don't try to touch your knee to the floor. Instead, go down only as far as you can and still feel in control of the situation.

Benefits: This is a great hip/thigh firmer because it uses all your thigh muscles (especially rectus femoris), your hip flexor muscles, and your ankle, feet, calf, and shin muscles too. You can vary the exercise to suit your individual needs: to work on the top of your thigh, point your toes straight ahead; to work on the inner thighs, turn your toes in; to work on the outsides of your thighs, turn your toes out.

Position: Stand properly: fanny under, belly tight, back straight, shoulders relaxed. Place your hands on your hips.

Procedure

1. Step forward with your left foot.

2. Bend your right knee, and try to touch it to the floor. (If that's too difficult, go only as far down as you can comfortably.)

3. Rise to standing position again by using the muscles in your legs to push you up; don't push against your left thigh with your hands.

4. Step forward with your right foot, and try to touch your left knee to the floor.

   More Difficult: Either take more steps this way, or repeat step 1, but instead of touching your knee to the floor, go almost all the way to the floor and stop there. Then rise a *little* bit, and sink almost to the floor again. Keep rising and sinking, and, when your legs feel tired, come all the way up, and change legs.

#42. Squat Stretch

Cautions and Hints: Another exercise that can bother bad knees. Keep your knees open wide; don't allow them to roll in as that increases the strain on your hip and knee joints.

Benefits: This is truly an allover exercise, and it just happens to be especially good for hips and thighs. You'll be using the front thigh muscles, the back thigh muscles, your fanny muscles, the muscles in your calves and ankles and feet, and some of your back muscles as well. You'll be strengthening thighs and fanny, stretching hamstrings, inner thighs, and pelvic floor muscles. It's a good delivery exercise.

Position: Squat down on your feet, feet pointing at a 45° angle to the sides, heels on the floor. Open your knees wide and, using thigh muscles, push them back until they are directly over your feet. Place your hands on the floor, between your legs. Your hands should be about 12 inches apart, with fingers spread. (Do your knees bother you here? Then this exercise isn't for you, yet.) Keep your belly tight.

Procedure

1. Keep your knees back over your feet, and slowly raise your fanny—keep pushing your knees back—until your legs are as straight as possible (no locked knees, of course).

2. Try to keep your knees over your feet and slowly lower your fanny until you return to starting position.

More Difficult: Repeat step 1. If you can straighten your legs completely without strain, and if your knees are strong, straighten your legs, then give a small hop. Complete exercise as above.

11
Special Exercises for Strengthening Weak Places

*A*ll along I've been harping at you: *strengthen* those weak body parts before you do anything too strenuous. Don't do *this* until your knees are strong. Don't do *that* if your ankles are bad. Make your feet strong *first*. Don't do this until your *wrists* are strong. Nag. Nag. Nag.

So, you have every right to demand that I give you some exercises for strengthening those weak places. Here they are.

These exercises are good, fundamental strengtheners for dealing with most of the weak-body problems that *I* encounter. If you have some other physical weakness that is not dealt with in this section or some other one, your doctor should have some good suggestions for dealing with it. The chart at the end of this chapter refers to exercises included elsewhere in the book that are also good, fundamental strengtheners.

Now, if your body is pretty strong and fit and you don't have any places that regularly protest, you don't even have to look at this chapter. But, if you have bad knees, or weak wrists, or aching feet, *do* take a look at the appropriate exercises. And, then, if they feel like something you ought to be doing, *do* them. Twice a day (at least) to start. After you've become stronger, incorporate them in your regular exercise routine and do them three times a week.

#43.   Knee Pushes

Cautions and Hints: Second only to bad backs, and running neck to neck with bad shoulders, are bad knees. Hundreds of people have trouble with their knees. Part of the problem is that people who remain inactive develop soft, weak thigh muscles, and thigh muscles compose the bulk of support for knee joints. This exercise will help strengthen inner and outer thigh muscles and will help make your knee a more reliable joint. You should also work with your rectus femoris (front thigh muscle—see #44, Knee Lifts).

Benefits: Strengthens weak knees by strengthening inner and outer thigh muscles, as well as other muscles surrounding the knee joint.

Position: Sit in a chair with your feet flat on the floor, and well apart. Lean forward and rest your elbows on your upper thighs. Place your left palm against the inside of your right knee. Place your right hand over your left hand.

Procedure

1. Press your right knee hard against your hands. At the same time press your hands hard against your knee.
2. Hold for a slow count of 5.
3. Release. Then repeat steps 1−2.
4. Now, place your left palm on the *out*side of your right knee. Place your right hand over your left.
5. Repeat step 1.
6. Repeat steps 2−3.
7. Then repeat the entire sequence with your left knee. (Reverse your hands so that your right palm is against your left knee.)

   More Difficult: Not necessary. Other exercises involving thigh muscles are now appropriate.

#44. Knee Lifts

Cautions and Hints: If your knee bothers you right beneath your knee bone, go back to Knee Pushes (#43) for a while.

Benefits: Strengthens weak knees by strengthening the rectus femoris muscle.

Position: Sit on a chair with your feet flat on the floor. Tie a weight bag around your right ankle. If you don't have a weight bag, tuck a salt container full of sand or a can of vegetables into a knee-high sock and tie that around your ankle. Begin with approximately 1½ pounds.

Procedure

1. Keeping your upper leg still, slowly raise your foot until it is the same height as your thigh.
2. Hold for a slow count of 5.
3. Slowly lower your foot.
4. Repeat steps 1−3.
5. Repeat entire sequence with your left foot.

   More Difficult: Increase the weight.

#45. Hand Strengtheners

Cautions and Hints: Superwoman you won't become by doing this exercise. But I guarantee that you'll be able to cope with any pickle jar you happen to run across. If your hands are extremely weak and this causes them to ache, do the exercise with your hands submerged in warm water.

Position: In any comfortable position, hold a tennis ball in your right hand.

Procedure

1. Squeeze that tennis ball as hard as you can. Count slowly to 5.
2. Relax.
3. Repeat with left hand.

More Difficult: Sporting goods stores sell hand squeezers designed to strengthen hands. Get one and squeeze away.

#46. Wrist Strengtheners

Cautions and Hints: There is absolutely no point in not being able to do many fun and necessary things because your wrists give out on you. This is a simple exercise and you can do it almost anywhere.

Benefits: Strengthens wrists. You will also be using your forearm muscles.

Position: In any comfortable position, hold a one-pound weight (or a can of peas or a book) in each hand.

Procedure

1. With the palms of your hands facing up, move your hands in every possible direction.
2. Repeat with your palms facing down.

More Difficult: Increase the weight.

#47. Pectoral Muscle Strengthener and Stretcher

Cautions and Hints: The first part of this exercise strengthens the pectoral muscles in your chest, the second part stretches them. Be careful during the second part to keep your head still—"goosenecking" (forward/backward movement) can pull neck muscles.

Benefits: This exercise works primarily on the pectoral muscles, those muscles underlying your breasts. Some pregnant women, especially those with naturally big breasts, complain of chest discomfort. This is sometimes caused by increased breast weight pulling on the supporting ligaments and musculature. And so, by increasing the strength of the pectoral muscles, it is possible to have them assist the ligaments and thereby ease the discomfort. (A good bra helps too.) Also involved in this exercise are the deltoid muscles, the trapezius muscles, and the rhomboideus muscles (they pull your shoulders back).

Position: Sit tailor fashion or stand in proper posture. (Place your feet apart for balance if you stand.) Place the palms of your hands together, perpendicular to each other (make an "L" shape with your hands). Keep your hands and elbows at shoulder level.

Procedure

1. Inhale.
2. As you exhale, press the palms of your hands together—hard.
3. Breathe normally, and hold for a slow count of 5.
4. Release and repeat steps 1–3.
5. Now, extend your arms straight out to the sides. Breathe normally for the rest of the exercise.
6. *Gently* push them straight back (at shoulder level still).
7. Slowly count to 3.
8. Release, and repeat steps 6–7.

#48.   Arm Slides

Cautions and Hints: Be sure to keep your shoulder blades, wrists, and elbows against the wall at all times.

Benefits: This is a good exercise for correcting rounded shoulders. It strengthens the postural muscles (rhomboideus) between your shoulder blades, and stretches your pectoral muscles.

Position: Sit in tailor fashion with your back against a wall. Extend your arms to the sides at shoulder level, with your elbows bent and your forearms pointing straight up. Place your shoulder blades, elbows, wrists, and the backs of your hands against the wall, and *keep* them there. Keep your belly tight.

Procedure

1. Keeping everything against the wall, slowly slide your right arm up the wall until it is straight.
2. Slowly slide it back down again.
3. Repeat steps 1–2 with your left arm.

More Difficult: Hold weight bags in your hands.

#49. Toe Curls

Cautions and Hints: People usually take their feet for granted. But if you have ever had sore, aching feet, you already understand why it is so important to take care of them. They must work all day long, every day, carrying your weight around, and they deserve some attention. Do this exercise barefooted, and do it often.

Benefits: This strengthens the muscles along the long arch of your foot, and those along the bottom of your toes. It stretches the muscles on the top of your toes. It is especially good for people with flat feet. You'll hear over and over again that there's nothing that can be done about flat feet. And it is true that it's pretty hard to do anything about the bones. But you can work with the muscles, and by doing that, relieve a lot of the aching and tiredness. Besides that, this is a fantastic exercise for developing toe control. Don't laugh—toe control comes in real handy when you have a baby in one arm, a telephone in the other hand, and you've just dropped your pencil.

Position: Take off your shoes and socks. Sit in a straight-backed chair. Let your feet rest comfortably on the floor.

Procedure

1. Make tight "fists" with your toes.
2. Hold for a slow count of 5.
3. Relax.
4. Repeat steps 1–3.

More Difficult: Do the exercise as outlined above. But after step 2, keep the fists and roll onto the outside edges of your feet. Hold that. When that's too easy, stand up and do the exercise. Then, place a couple of marbles on the floor, pick them up with your toes, and do the exercise.

#50. Foot Stretches

Cautions and Hints: Flat-footed people often have trouble convincing their feet that they really can do this—just keep going. After all, who's boss—you or your feet?

Benefits: This stretches the muscles in the long arch of your foot, as well as the muscles on the ball of your foot and on the bottom of your toes.

Position: Take off your shoes and socks and sit in a straight-backed chair. Place your toes directly under your knees. Make sure that your heels touch the floor.

Procedure

1. Lift your heels until you are "standing" on the balls of your feet and your toes.

2. Push the front/top of your foot as far over your toes as you can.

3. Hold for a slow count of 5.

4. Slowly return to starting position.

   More Difficult: Do Calf Stretch and Strengthener (#51).

#51. Calf Stretch and Strengthener

Cautions and Hints: More women than men suffer from tight calf muscles and Achilles tendons. That's because so many of us have been lured into believing that it is more important to wear stylish shoes than sensible ones. By sensible shoes I don't mean the kind of sturdy brown oxfords that those of us with foot problems wore as kids, but I do mean shoes with low heels and good support. High-heeled shoes, appropriately named, keep heels higher than toes, and if worn often enough result in shortened calf muscles and tendons. If you feel uncomfortable in your calf area or the back of your heels when you are barefooted or wearing sneakers, then you probably have worn high heels too long and have shortened heel cords and calf muscles. If that is the case, ditch those high-heeled shoes right now and get into something that is healthier for your feet and legs (and back, too, remember).

Benefits: This exercise stretches the calf muscles and Achilles tendons. It strengthens them too, as well as the muscles running up your shins. It makes calves more shapely to boot.

Position: Stand facing the back of a chair (or a table, or a wall). Place a two-by-four on the floor in back of the chair. Place your heels on the floor, and the balls of your feet on the board. Rest your hands lightly on the back of the chair for balance.

Procedure

1. Relax into this stretching position, and hold it for about a minute.

2. Step off the board, if your calf muscles and heel cords are very tight.

3. If you feel relatively comfortable with step 1, skip step 2.

4. Then slowly rise up until you are standing on the balls of your feet and your toes.

5. Hold for a slow count of 5.

6. Slowly lower your heels until they touch the floor again.

7. Repeat steps 1−5.

   More Difficult: Increase the height of the board. When that's no longer a challenge, place the balls of your feet on a step and let your heels hang down. Do the exercise as directed.

Basic Strengtheners*

Body Part	# of Exercise	Name of Exercise	Page #
Neck	1	Neck Rolls (difficult)	27
	11	Roll-Ups	40
Shoulders	13	Wall Push-Ups	43
	20	Thumbs Down	61
Chest (Bosom)	13	Wall Push-Ups	43
	20	Thumbs Down	61
	47	Pectoral Muscle Strengthener and Stretch	108
Upper Arms	13	Wall Push-Ups	43
	20	Thumbs Down	61
Wrists	13	Wall Push-Ups	43
	46	Wrist Strengtheners	108
Hands	45	Hand Strengtheners	107
Front Abdominals	10	Pelvic Tilt	39
	11	Roll-Ups	40
Lateral Abdominals	7	Lateral Bends	36
	27	Side Torso Raises	74
Upper Back	20	Thumbs Down	61
	13	Wall Push-Ups	43
	30	Angry Cat	85
Lower Back	10	Pelvic Tilt	39
	11	Roll-Ups	40
	34	Lower Back Stretch	91
Buttocks	14	The Doggy	44
	35	Leg Extensions (back)	94
	36	String of Beads	97
Thighs			
Front	35	Leg Extensions (front)	94
	41	Kneeling Walk (toes straight ahead)	103
Back	35	Leg Extensions (back)	103
	36	String of Beads	97
Inside	39	Inner Thigh Lifts	100
	41	Kneeling Walk (pigeon-toed)	103
Outside	14	The Doggy	44
	35	Leg Extensions (side)	103
	41	Kneeling Walk (toes out)	103
Calves	51	Calf Stretch and Strengthener	111
Ankles	5	Ankle Circles	33
	15	Ankle Rolls	50
Feet	49	Toe Curls	110
	50	Foot Stretches	110

*I've included only two or three of the most basic strengtheners for each category. For a more complete list of exercises according to body parts, see Appendix B.

12
Exercises for Childbirth

*I*n a very real sense, all the calisthenics in this book are exercises for childbirth because they make your total body fitter and stronger. But, some of the calisthenics *do* work more on the body parts most involved with delivery—primarily pelvic floor, abdomen, and lower back and, secondarily, inner thighs, and shoulders/arms—than do others. I'm including a brief list here. There are exercise books specifically designed for preparing women for childbirth. See the reading list included in Chapter 15.

Please refer to pages listed for complete instructions for each exercise.

Pg. #	# of Exercise	Name of Exercise	Delivery Benefits
	9	Inner Thigh Stretch	Stretches inner thighs and pelvic floor. Increases lower back flexibility.
	10	Pelvic Tilt	Strengthens front abdominals, lower back, pelvic floor. Increases pelvic flexibility.
	11	Roll-Ups	Strengthens front abdominals. Stretches lower back.
	12	Pelvic Floor Strengtheners	Strengthens pelvic floor. Teaches relaxation of pelvic floor.
	13	Wall Push-Ups	Strengthens shoulders and upper arms so that they won't become tired during the pushing stage of labor.
	29	Straddle Stretch	Stretches inner thighs, pelvic floor, and lower backs. Strengthens lateral abdominals and lower back.

Pg. #	# of Exercise	Name of Exercise	Delivery Benefits
	30	Angry Cat	Strengthens and stretches front abdominals and lower back. Increases spinal and pelvic flexibility. Strengthens pelvic floor.
	42	Squat Stretch	Stretches inner thighs and pelvic floor. Stretches buttocks and lower back.
		Aerobics	Improves cardiovascular and lung function. Builds stamina and endurance.

13
Relaxation

*T*he ability to make your body completely relax at your command is one of the most valuable tools you can cultivate. It can be used to help you fall asleep, to ward off depression, to rid your body and mind of unnecessary tension, and to get through even the roughest of days amazingly intact. In fact, if relaxation is practiced often enough and well enough, it can even replace sleep on occasion. I had a friend in college who was working nights—eight hours—and taking a full course load during the day. How did he do it? By relaxation. He could relax completely, instantly. And he could stay completely relaxed until his inner alarm system told him it was time to rouse himself. He catnapped like this whenever he had the chance—all day and all night long. And he made it through college with his health, his good humor, a very respectable grade point average, and many friends-turned-converts.

I have never given up what some people view as indulgence and I view as necessity—my twenty-minute afternoon rest. I started it in college, under my friend's supervision, and, after getting the hang of his relaxation technique, have used it ever since. It has helped keep me sane and healthy, even during periods when practically everything else seemed to be conspiring against my physical and mental health. Although I never have been able to develop my relaxation technique to the fine art that my friend's was, it has served me well nevertheless. I especially appreciated it when I was struggling to cope with the demands of a newborn who either slept all day but doggedly remained awake all night (that was Heather), or who slept regularly, but never for more than two hours at a time (Michael). It was then that I regularly offered silent little prayers of thanks to my friend for his wonderful gift of relaxation.

There's nothing very mystical about relaxation. Nor is it difficult to learn. But, like most skills of value, it takes practice. And, at first, quiet.

Your goals are simple ones. First, you will want to be able to tell when your muscles are contracted or slightly tensed and when they are relaxed. Second, you will eventually want to be able to relax those muscles just by wishing it so. And third, you will want to be able to relax your mind, so that thoughts drift in and out like dreams, and so that peripheral distractions (noise, etc.) no longer distract you.

Here's how to start. First, either reread the following instructions until you have memorized them (it's hard to relax when you must look at a book continually), or tape record them so that you can play them back, or have someone read them to you as you practice relaxation. Second, choose a comfortable position (see the illustrations in this chapter for examples). Close your eyes. Begin breathing deeply (abdominal breathing is best—as you inhale slowly, allow your belly to rise, as you exhale slowly your belly will fall), slowly and regularly. The beginning exercise follows. And, third, allow yourself at least twenty quiet uninterrupted minutes in which to relax.

1. As you inhale (deeply and slowly), tighten the muscles in your feet.
2. As you exhale (deeply and slowly), relax your feet.
3. As you inhale, tighten the muscles in your legs.
4. As you exhale, relax your legs completely.
5. As you inhale, tighten your pelvic floor muscles, and your buttocks.
6. As you exhale, completely relax your pelvic floor and buttocks.
7. As you inhale, tighten your belly muscles.
8. As you exhale, relax your belly completely.
9. As you inhale, tighten the muscles in your arms, shoulders and hands.
10. As you exhale, completely relax your arms, shoulders and hands.
11. As you inhale, tighten the muscles in your neck, your jaws, and your face.
12. As your exhale, completely relax your neck, your jaws, your face.
13. As you inhale, tighten your tongue against the roof of your mouth.
14. As you exhale, relax your tongue.
15. As you inhale, tighten your eyes and forehead.
16. As you exhale, relax your eyes and forehead.
17. Now inhale deeply.
18. As you exhale, completely relax your entire body. Breathe the words, "My body is heavy." Let your body sink right *through* the floor.
19. Breathe deeply and regularly and slowly, and each time you exhale try to relax completely. If you feel totally relaxed, you don't need to work through steps 20–29. Just keep breathing deeply! Relax. If you do not feel completely relaxed, continue with steps 20–29.
20. Inhale, and as you exhale, tell your feet to relax again.
21. Inhale, and as you exhale, tell your legs to relax again.
22. Inhale, and as you exhale, tell your pelvic floor and buttocks muscles to relax again.
23. Inhale, and as you exhale, tell your belly muscles to relax.
24. Inhale, and as you exhale, tell your arms and shoulders to relax completely.
25. Inhale, and as you exhale, tell your neck, your jaws, and your face to relax completely.
26. Inhale, and as you exhale, tell your tongue to relax.
27. Inhale, and as you exhale, relax your eyes and forehead.
28. Inhale, and as you exhale, relax your entire body.
29. Keep breathing deeply and slowly and relax completely with each exhalation. When it is time to get up again, do so slowly and gently. Give your body time to slowly come out of its state of relaxation.
30. Wiggle your fingers and toes.

31. Give a good, long stretch.

32. Open your eyes, and focus on something.

33. When you feel ready—not before—gently rise.

There! That's all there is to it. Practice that exercise regularly, and you will find that you are soon able to relax whenever you wish.

It's possible to embroider upon that exercise, to add little frills that make it an effective technique in self-hypnosis.

One such embroidery is to follow the instructions above and allow yourself to sink deeply into the state of relaxation. Then using your imagination, create a place for yourself that represents peace and serenity. Imagine the sounds of the place. The smells. The tastes. The feel. Imagine these things in as much detail as you can. If there is anyone with you in your secret place, imagine that person as clearly as possible. Now, imagine yourself in that place. You look fantastic. You are doing something you love doing. You feel happy and peaceful and satisfied. Imagine how your skin feels; if you are "outside," imagine how the wind or the sun or the rain feels on your body. Muster as much detail about everything as you can. And keep imagining until you feel relaxed and serene and full of peaceful thoughts.

Once you have created such a place for yourself, it is possible to retreat to that place whenever you need to. My secret place is a beach, much like the one I loved as a child. Just thinking about it brings me instant joy and peace. And I sneak away to that mind-beach whenever I am tired or sad or frustrated or depressed. It always helps me relax and rejuvenate.

Another frill is one that I use when I know that the day ahead is going to be a rough one. I don't know quite how this works, but it does work—it almost always helps me get through those days with good grace and good humor.

Allow yourself to sink into a state of deep relaxation. Then begin imagining the day ahead in as much detail as possible. Imagine yourself doing the chores for the day. You are shopping and enjoying the process. Your baby is crying and you are reacting with patience and love. You are cooking dinner, and humming happily as you do it. Keep going. Imagine every unpleasant chore ahead, but imagine it pleasantly, and imagine yourself full of goodwill and happiness at all times. Then, rouse yourself. As you plod through the day, you will probably find yourself reacting to expected situations in the way you imagined them. When that happens, and you're pleased with your fortitude and strength, give yourself a big mental pat on the back—you deserve it. And by acknowledging your success, you will make it that much easier for yourself to fall into these happy behavior patterns next time.

There it is. All I know about relaxation in a nutshell. There are many people more versed in this wonderful technique, and there are many books on the subject. If it intrigues you, find those people, get those books. Time spent in acquiring this skill is unfailingly well rewarded.

The following illustrations are examples of relaxing postures. Study them, try them out, and find one or two that meet your needs and will work for you. Or create your own. (Two other positions that work well for relaxation are illustrated in chapter 14, Feet High [#55] and Feet Higher [#56].)

#52. Side Sleeping

Even though the positions in this and the next sections were described in chapter 10, they are important enough to repeat here.

This method of resting or sleeping will eliminate strain on your lower back.

Lie on your side, with your knees bent and pulled close to your belly. (This rounds your lower back, and allows it to relax.)

Now, put a pillow between your knees to prevent the weight of your upper leg from pulling your lower back muscles on that side. Put another pillow under your head, and, if you wish, a small one under your belly to support *that*. And maybe one behind your back.

Close your eyes, and practice the relaxation exercise—breathing deeply and relaxing with each exhalation.

#53. Back Sleeping

Sleeping or resting on your back with your legs out straight causes your lower back to arch slightly, and can contribute to back discomfort. So try this variation instead.

Lie on your back, but put a pillow or two underneath your knees. This will round your lower back, and it will be completely supported.

Practice your relaxation exercise in this position.

#54.   Slumping Forward

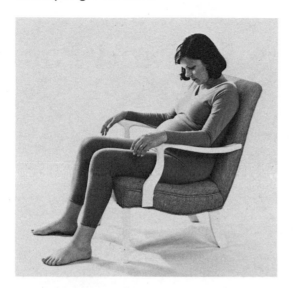

Since it is not always possible to sneak away and lie down whenever you are tired or tense, it is important to find an upright (almost) position that will allow you to relax and release tension.

This position works well for me—in between workshops, before speaking engagements, or while I'm typing. It is especially good for relieving tension in upper backs, necks, and shoulders, and helps relieve headaches or upper backaches. Plus, it is one time when slouching is exactly what you want to do.

Sit in a chair with armrests. Let your arms rest comfortably on the armrests. Place your feet well apart and flat on the floor. Let your belly relax. Allow your head to sink forward and your shoulders to round.

Now, try that relaxation exercise, and remember to try to relax everything each time you exhale.

14

Relief from Aches and Pains

*L*et's face it—pregnancy is not always comfortable. Especially during the last trimester. Too often backs ache and legs throb.

It's not necessary to be stoic and put up with these aches and pains. There are many things you can do to make yourself more comfortable.

The first thing to do is to increase your body awareness so that you can feel such discomfort sneaking up on you. Then you can do something about it right then, before it has a chance to really get you.

ACHING LEGS

Aching legs are generally caused by increased pressure in the leg veins, and, often, by water retention as well. Standing up only aggravates the problem, so you'll want to sit or lie down whenever you have the chance. If you are retaining water, it is a good idea to lie down often—bed rest causes any body to lose excess water. And drink plenty of water. And eat natural foods containing little sodium.

The following positions are good ones to use when you have the chance to rest.

#55. Feet High

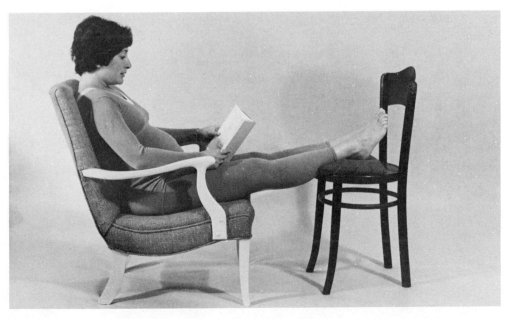

Whenever you have a chance to sit down, try to elevate your legs.

Sit in a comfortable chair. If necessary, put a small pillow behind your lower back to support it. Then put your feet on anything that is higher than the seat of the chair you're sitting in. That will allow gravity to help move blood out of your legs so that it doesn't pool there.

Do this as often as possible—when you're reading or reading to your children, when you're talking on the telephone or chatting with friends, when you're on your coffee break, when you're peeling carrots, etc.

#56. Feet Higher

This is an absolutely wonderful way to take a breather.

Lie on the floor, with a pillow under your head, and one under your hips. Then prop your feet on the back of a chair, a table, the wall, or anything else that will get them up high.

In this position, your back is completely supported, and gravity helps the blood flow out of your legs. If you begin to feel light-headed or anxious, roll to your side—your baby may be compressing major blood vessels.

Aching Back

Backs ache during pregnancy for a number of reasons. If your doctor has said that your backaches are muscular in origin, then you should be strengthening your abdominal muscles, stretching and strengthening your back muscles, and trying to stand and sit properly.

But sometimes your back aches even when you're doing all these things. Then, it's time to help your back relax, to get rid of tension that you might be carrying there.

I've found the following positions helpful in relieving aching backs.

#57. Lower Back Stretch

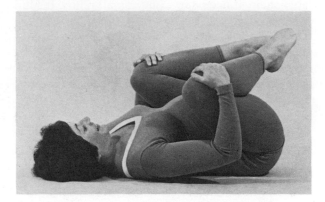

This was included in the section on exercises for the back, but I'm including it here as well because it really does feel good when your back is sore.

Lie on the floor on your back. Cross your ankles. Clasp your knees with your hands. Gently pull your knees to the outside of your belly and as close to your shoulders as you can. This will help relax those tight back muscles.

#58. Hamstring Stretch

You'll remember this exercise from the Regular Calisthenic Exercise Routine. But it's also effective as a back relaxer.

Stand upright, with your belly tight. Gently bend forward as far as you comfortably can. Let your head relax. Let your arms and shoulders relax. Now, just hang there, breathing deeply and regularly. When you're ready to come up again, do so slowly so that you don't become dizzy. And bend your knees as you rise.

These positions will only provide temporary relief. They won't cure your aching legs or back. But sometimes temporary relief is all you'll need.

→

Models with their babies. *From left to right:* Susie Richardson, with her son, Andrew, 6 weeks old; Carol Whiteley, with her son, Mark, 5 months old; Lynne Morrall, with her daughter, Alexandra, 5 months old; Jill Phillips, with her son, Scott, 4 months old; and Jan Mangione, with her son, Peter, 10 months old.

15
You May Want to Know About . . .

THE MODELS

I just finished looking once more at the photographs that I took for this book, and it is interesting to me that the women who modeled for the book look like, well, *models*. In fact, they aren't. They are women who joined my fitness class during their pregnancies, and who happened to be close to delivery about the time I needed to take photographs. (They are also wonderful human beings who gave freely of their time for photographic sessions, and who supported me with a great deal of loving energy.)

I chose to include several women as models because I wanted to illustrate how very different women's bodies can look and still be beautiful. I have become aware, over the years, of how discontented most of us are with our bodies. I suppose a big part of that comes from the cultural indoctrination that says that in order for a woman's body to be considered beautiful it must be lean, long-legged, and big-breasted. But I think that *all* the women who modeled for my book have beautiful bodies. And, as you can see, they are very different. Susie is not even five feet tall. Lynne, on the other hand, stands about five feet seven inches. Carol, Jill, and Jan are in the five feet three inch to five feet five inch range. They have very different bone structures, very different proportions, and like most of us, each one has something about her body that she wishes were different. But as I look at these women, I see much beauty, and, as a result, am becoming much more accepting of my own body. I hope that you will experience that same increased self-acceptance.

I'd like to introduce each of them very briefly.

Jan Mangione had been jogging on a regular basis before she came to class in her first trimester of pregnancy. She was a faithful participant in the class throughout her pregnancy, and even though her labor was long (twenty hours), she recovered quickly, and felt good after her delivery. Her son, Peter, is her first child, and he was 8 pounds when he was born. Jan was 9 months pregnant when the photos were taken.

Lynne Morrall also came to class early in her pregnancy, even though she was working full time, and had to take her lunch break at 9:00 A.M. to fit the class in. In the photographs you may notice that there are strap marks on her feet from her shoes. That was because Lynne was retaining a lot of water. The photographs were taken when she was in her eighth month of pregnancy, and the water retention continued to be a problem for the rest of her pregnancy. She had a long labor, and eventually, because her baby was in breech position, had a cesarean birth. Alexandra is her first child and weighed 7 pounds 6 ounces at birth. Lynne was back in class about a month after the baby was born.

Jill Phillips was also in her eighth month when her photographs were taken. She started the class in her middle trimester, and because of her job, could not come each time. She came quite regularly, however, feeling that it was a good psychic as well as physical experience. Jill's water broke several hours before she went to the hospital. Because she had not yet gone into labor, she was given medication to induce labor. She delivered her first child, Scott, five hours later. He was 7 pounds 13 ounces.

Susie Richardson first came to my class when she was pregnant with her first child, Laren, who is now almost two years old, and she just never quit coming. She was in her ninth month of pregnancy with her second baby when the photographs were taken. She is one of those lucky women who has very short labors. Laren was born about three hours after her labor began, and Andrew, who was 6 pounds 13 ounces at birth, was born in less than two hours. She was back in class two weeks after Andrew was born and is still going strong.

Carol Whiteley was in her eighth month of pregnancy when the photographs were taken. Mark is her first child, and weighed 7 pounds 4½ ounces when he was born. Her labor lasted twenty-one hours. Carol came back to class when Mark was about a month old, and continued until he was three months old, when she went back to work.

ORGANIZATIONS

The following organizations are dedicated to the health, education, and welfare of pregnant women and their mates. I do not have personal knowledge of many of them, and, therefore, cannot endorse them. I offer them to you as resources for obtaining information in many areas of pregnancy, childbirth, and parenting.

THE AMERICAN ACADEMY OF HUSBAND-COACHED CHILDBIRTH
P.O. Box 5224,
Sherman Oaks, California 91413

This organization provides literature, films, teacher training, and information pertaining to the Bradley method of childbirth education. Information of local classes.

AMERICAN NATIONAL RED CROSS
National Headquarters
Washington, D.C. 20006

Offers Preparation for Parenthood, Health in the Home, Standard First Aid and Personal Safety, Cardiopulmonary Resuscitation, and other educational and health courses. Contact your local Red Cross chapter for further information.

ASSOCIATION FOR CHILDBIRTH AT HOME, INTERNATIONAL (ACAH)
P.O. Box 1219
Cerritos, California 90701

This nationwide organization offers classes for parents who want to have their children born at home, an intensive certification program for ACAH leaders to teach the parent classes, as well as an Advanced Leader Training Program for leaders who want to be midwives. Publishes a newsletter, "BirthNotes," and has an international referral service of professional and lay resources for home birth.

C/SEC
c/o Melissa Foley
15 Maynard Road
Dedham, Massachusetts 02026

Information, education, and support for parents who are anticipating a cesarean delivery or who have experienced one. Has publications list. Write for information about groups in your area that support cesarean parents.

CHILDREN IN HOSPITALS
31 Wilshire Park
Needham, Massachusetts 02192

Provides education about the needs of children and parents for continued and ample contact when either is hospitalized. Encourages hospitals to adopt flexible visiting policies and to provide living-in accommodations whenever possible. Offers personal counseling, a newsletter, information sheets, a 1974 survey of Boston-area hospital policies toward visiting and rooming in. There is a fee for the survey.

*COUNTY HEALTH DEPARTMENTS

Services may vary from place to place. In California, for example, the services are free and include Well Baby/Immunization Clinics, Crippled Children's Services, Dental Care Clinics (for those under 18 years of age), Pregnancy Testing and Prenatal Care, Family Planning, and many others. Check with your local health department to see what they offer.

HOME ORIENTED MATERNITY EXPERIENCE (H.O.M.E.)
P.O. Box 20852
Milwaukee, Wisconsin 53220

Offers information, support, and encouragement to families interested in home birth. Their publication *Home Oriented Maternity Experience: A Comprehensive Guide to Home Birth* is an excellent resource for those seriously considering home birth. It discusses, thoroughly and well, both the pros and cons of home birth. There is a fee for this publication.

INTERNATIONAL CHILDBIRTH EDUCATION ASSOCIATION (ICEA)
P.O. Box 20852
Milwaukee, Wisconsin 53220

Focuses upon many aspects of family-centered maternity care. Provides information about local chapters, activities, etc.

INTERNATIONAL CHILDBIRTH EDUCATION ASSOCIATION SUPPLIES CENTER
P.O. Box 70258
Seattle, Washington 98107

Source of books and publications on prepared childbirth, infant feeding, parenting, etc. Publishes *Bookmarks,* which comes out three times a year, and which contains book lists and reviews. It is an excellent resource for professionals or other persons interested in keeping abreast of current lay literature in pregnancy, childbirth, and related areas.

LA LECHE LEAGUE, INTERNATIONAL
9616 Minneapolis Avenue
Franklin Park, Illinois 60131

Dedicated to helping women breastfeed their children. Publishes their manual *The Womanly Art of Breastfeeding,* bimonthly *News,* and numerous information sheets. Write for information about La Leche League branches in your area, or for breastfeeding Hot Lines.

NATIONAL ASSOCIATION FOR RETARDED CITIZENS
2709 Avenue E, East
Arlington, Texas 76011

Helps parents of retarded children, professionals in the mental retardation field, and mentally retarded persons share problems and solutions. Prevention of mental retardation as it relates to adequate prenatal care is a major concern. Also raises funds for better facilities, research, and treatment of mental retardation. Will answer any inquiries and supply pertinent information.

THE NATIONAL FOUNDATION—March of Dimes
1275 Mamaroneck Avenue
White Plains, New York 10605

Goals: prevention of birth defects and any life-threatening condition in the newborn. Health education materials available upon request.

*NATIONAL FOUNDATION FOR SUDDEN INFANT DEATH
1501 Broadway
New York, New York 10036

Offers information about sudden infant death syndrome, and solace to parents. Write for information and for local chapters.

*NATIONAL ORGANIZATION OF MOTHERS OF TWINS CLUB
5402 Amberwood Lane
Rockville, Maryland 20353

Offers information and support as well as helpful hints for mothers of twins. Write for information and for chapters in your area.

*"PREGNANT PATIENTS' BILL OF RIGHTS"
Committee of Patient Rights
Box 1900
New York, New York 10001

Discusses the legal rights of pregnant patients as they pertain to medical care, hospitalization, etc. Free. Send self-addressed stamped envelope.

THE PREMATURE AND HIGH RISK INFANT ASSOCIATION
Box A—3083
Peoria, Illinois 61614

Provides emotional and educational support to the parent(s) of premature and/or high risk infants. Offers a twenty-four-hour Help Line (309) 688-0274, a hospital visitor program, and various pertinent publications. One booklet informs parents about the nursery, answers common questions about premature and high risk infants, offers emotional support, and includes sections on home hints, financial aid, etc. Write for information.

*These organizations have not answered my inquiries, so I do not have approval for use of this text. I have written permission to include all other information.

SUGGESTED READING

I've enjoyed the books I've listed here, and hope that you will find them both informative and helpful.

Whenever possible, I have included information about the price of the books, and (in the parentheses) the Dewey Decimal call numbers to help you find the books easily in your public library. Some of the call numbers may vary from library to library, so if you don't find the book(s) you're looking for on the shelves, check the card catalogue.

It is also possible to have your librarian obtain a book that your library doesn't own—either by an Inter-Library Loan, or by outright purchase. Ask them about that.

Also, *Books in Print* (in the reference section of the library) has all information about most of the books listed here. It will not, however, contain information about publications put out by organizations rather than publishers. Nevertheless, *Books in Print* has addresses for all publishing houses. You can order books directly from the publisher or have a local bookstore order them for you.

The asterisks refer to books that I highly recommend.

Good reading!

PREGNANCY

Fetal development

Flanagan, Geraldine. *The First Nine Months of Life*. Simon and Schuster, 1962, $6.95 (612.6F).

The development of a baby from conception to birth. Story told in words and pictures.

*Ingelman-Sundberg, and Wirsen, Claus, et al. *A Child Is Born: The Drama of Life Before Birth*. Delacorte Press, 1966, $9.95, Dell Publishing Company, 1969, $3.95 (612.6N).

A beautifully photographed revelation of human reproduction from conception to birth.

Maternity Center Association. *A Baby Is Born,* 3rd Edition, Grosset & Dunlap, 1964, $4.95 (618M).

Shows prenatal development and the birth process through the use of sculptured models.

*Rugh, Roberts, et al. *From Conception to Birth: The Drama of Life's Beginnings*. Harper & Row, 1971, $13.50 (612.6R).

An excellent book with fine illustrations.

General

*Boston Children's Medical Center. *Pregnancy, Birth and the Newborn Baby: A Complete Guide for Parents and Parents to Be*. Delacorte Press, 1972, $10.00 (618B).

A highly readable, comprehensive guide written by experts in obstetrics and gynecology, pediatrics, psychiatry, child development, genetics, and nutrition.

*Boston Women's Health Collective. *Our Bodies, Ourselves: A Book by and for Women*. Revised 2nd Edition, Simon & Schuster, 1976, $9.95/$3.95 (q301.412B).

If there were any one general book about women's health and bodies that I think every woman should own, this is it. Although the section on childbirth is scant, the approach to anatomy and physiology of women is excellent. Illustrated.

*Colman, Arthur, and Coleman, Libby L. *Pregnancy: The Psychological Experience*. Seabury Press, Inc., 1972, $6.95 (612.6C).

Treats the feelings, anxieties, fears, and joys of the entire family. Discusses the normal psychological experience of pregnancy. Although the sample population is small, this is probably the best subjectively significant book on the psychology of pregnancy.

C/SEC, Inc. *Frankly Speaking: A Pamphlet for Cesarean Couples*. C/Sec, 1976, $3.00 (nonmembers), $1.50 (members)

A practical, helpful pamphlet dealing with hospital experiences, home care, and emotional self-help for cesarean couples. Obtain by writing to Melissa Foley, 15 Maynard Road, Dedham, Massachusetts 02026 or Anne Cornetta, 5 A Street, Belmont, Massachusetts 02178.

Marzollo, Jean. *Nine Months, One Day, One Year*. Harper & Row, 1975, $7.95/paper (649.1).

A book written by parents and edited by Marzollo, this is human, humorous, and contains lots of helpful hints.

*Noble, Elizabeth, *Essential Exercises for the Childbearing Year: A Guide to Health and Comfort Before and After Your Baby Is Born*. Houghton Mifflin Co., 1976, $10.95, also in paperback (618.2).

Noble discusses specific exercise in terms of providing preventative measures against possible gynecological or urinary problems later in life. Makes strong argument for women taking control of their bodies, and therefore provides thorough explanations of the birthing muscles—pelvic floor, abdominals— and their functions, as well as the postural muscles. Excellent discussion of these muscles, especially of the pelvic floor. Special chapters provide exercises to do during pregnancy and afterward, exercises for cesarean mothers. Excellent resource and reading list.

Salk, Lee. *Preparing for Parenthood: Understanding Your Feelings About Pregnancy, Childbirth, and Your Baby*. David McKay Co., Inc., 1974, $7.95, Bantam Press, 1975, $1.95 (649S).

Highly readable and entertaining. Deals with parental feelings toward pregnancy, childbirth, and babies.

Nutrition

Davis, Adelle. *Let's Have Healthy Children*. Harcourt Brace Jovanovich, Publishers, 1972, $6.95, New American Library, $1.95 (618.2D).

Good guide to maternal and infant nutrition, both during pregnancy and afterward. Somewhat controversial.

Fredericks, Carlton. *Psycho-Nutrition*. Grosset & Dunlap, 1976, $7.95 (616.891F).

It is Fredericks' contention that diet greatly affects one's psychological state. He gives guidelines for diet and vitamin supplements.

*Lappe, Francis Moore. *Diet for a Small Planet*. Revised Edition, Ballantine Books, Inc., 1975, $1.95 (641.5L).

Thought-provoking book about creating complete proteins without using meats. Includes many excellent recipes.

National Academy of Sciences. *Maternal Nutrition in the Course of Pregnancy,* 1970, 25¢.

A report from the Committee on Maternal Nutrition, Food and Nutrition Board, National Research Council. Available from your county nutritionist.

*Williams, Phyllis. *Nourishing Your Unborn Child: Nutrition and Natural Foods in Pregnancy*. Nash Publications, 1974, $7.95.

An excellent resource on prenatal nutrition.

Exercise and Relaxation

Bing, Elisabeth. *Moving through Pregnancy*. Bobbs-Merrill Co., Inc., 1975, $7.50/$4.50, Bantam Books, 1976, $1.95.

Many helpful hints for getting through pregnancy as comfortably as possible. Exercise program with photographs. (Avoid the leg lifts and straight-legged sit-ups she suggests.)

*Hartman, Rhondda E. *Exercises for a True Natural Childbirth*. Harper & Row, 1975, $9.95.

An excellent resource for good preparation-for-childbirth exercises.

Medvin, Jennine O'Brien. *Prenatal Yoga and Natural Birth*. Freestone Publishing Company, 1974, $2.50 (q618.24).

The photographed yoga positions are easy to understand and the line drawings are beautiful. The text is a bit mystical, though beautiful and well written.

Shepro, David, and Knuttgen, Howard. *Complete Conditioning: The No-Nonsense Guide to Fitness and Good Health*. Addison-Wesley, 1976, $6.95.

A valuable guide to aerobic (cardiovascular) fitness; plus information on nutrition, weight control, and many of the commercially available fitness gadgets.

*White, John, and Fadiman, James. *Relax: How You Can Feel Better, Reduce Stress, and Overcome Tension*. Dell/The Confucian Press, Inc., 1976, $1.95 paper.

One book that provides a thorough introduction to many relaxation techniques, excerpts from several authors, plus usable how-to tips. This book did not go into a second printing, but it is well worth writing directly to the publisher to obtain your copy.

Labor and Delivery

*Arms, Suzanne. *Immaculate Deception: A New Look at Women and Childbirth in America*. Houghton Mifflin Co., 1975, $11.95/$6.95 (618A).

This book looks critically at many routine birthing techniques. An important book in that it shows couples the choices that should be available to them for their birth experience.

*Bradley, Robert A. *Husband-Coached Childbirth*. Revised Edition, Harper & Row, 1974, $7.95/paper (618B).

The Bradley technique for natural childbirth. The husband's role is well defined.

Dick-Read, Grantly. *Childbirth without Fear: The Original Approach to Natural Childbirth*. 4th Edition, Harper & Row, 1972, $8.95 (618R).

Explains the Dick-Read technique for natural childbirth.

*Ewy, Donna, and Ewy, Roger. *Preparation for Childbirth*. Pruett Publishing Co., 1970, $5.50, New American Library, 1974, $1.50 (618E).

Easy-to-read, detailed explanation of the Lamaze method of prepared childbirth.

*Haire, Doris, and Haire, John. *The Cultural Warping of Childbirth*. International Childbirth Education Association, 1974, $1. Available from the I.C.E.A. Supplies Center. See the list of Organizations.

An important short book that questions many routine obstetrical practices, points out cultural differences in birthing practices, and possible choices for birthing couples.

*Hazell, Lester D. *Commonsense Childbirth*. G. P. Putnam's Sons, Tower Publications, Inc., 1972, $1.50 (618).

If I were to recommend any one book on childbirth preparation, this would be it. Hazell presents a good commonsense approach to childbirth.

*Home Oriented Maternity Experience. *Home Oriented Maternity Experience: A Comprehensive Guide to Home Birth*. Available from Home Oriented Maternity Experience, 511 New York Avenue, Washington, D.C. 20012. Write for price information.

An excellent resource that discusses pros and cons of home birth.

*Sousa, Marion. *Childbirth at Home*. Prentice-Hall International, Inc., 1976, $7.95 (618).

Well-researched, heavily footnoted, this is an excellent book for those planning to have their baby at home.

*Ward, Charlotte, and Ward, Fred. *The Home Birth Book*. Inscape Corporation, 1975, $14.50/$6.95.

Informative for people wishing home birth experience. Pediatrician, parents, midwife's, obstetrician's views of home birth are presented.

White, Gregory, M.D. *Emergency Childbirth*. Franklin Park, Illinois: Police Training Foundation, 1958.

Emphasizes the capability of the average female body to safely and effectively deliver a baby, and gives specific "how-to-assist" advice for the childbirth attendant. Highly recommended if you are planning a home birth.

PARENTING

Breastfeeding

*Eiger, Marvin, and Olds, Sally. *The Complete Book of Breastfeeding*. The Workman Publishing Company, Inc., 1972, $6.95, Bantam Books, 1973, $1.50 (618.92).

Comprehensive, easy to read. Includes "Sex and the Nursing Mother," and a section on problems and solutions.

*Ewy, Donna, and Ewy, Roger. *Preparation for Breastfeeding*. Doubleday, 1975, $2.95 (618.92).

This book details the physical and emotional advantages to breastfeeding. It is easy to read and has step-by-step photographs. Encouraging and supportive.

Gerand, Alice. *Please Breastfeed Your Baby*. Hawthorn Books, Inc., 1970, $4.95, Fomur International, 1975, 75¢.

A commonsense aproach to nursing. Compelling evidence of its value.

Haire, Doris. *Instructions for Nursing Your Baby*. Available through the I.C.E.A. Supplies Center, P.O. Box 70258, Seattle, Washington 98107, 25¢.
Short, practical, easy to read.

La Leche League International. *The Womanly Art of Breastfeeding*. Available through La Leche League International, 9616 Minneapolis Avenue, Franklin Park, Illinois 60131, $3 (618.92L).
The classic book of breastfeeding.

Child Care and Development

Banet, Barbara, and Rozdilsky, Mary L. *What Now? A Handbook for New Parents*. Scribner's, 1975, $7.95, also in paperback.
Buy this book *before* your baby comes. It contains a wealth of information on how to take care of *yourself*, rather than how to take care of the baby. Fine chapter on dealing with crying babies.

Brazelton, T. Barry. *Infants and Mothers: Differences in Development*. Delacorte Press, 1969, $10, Dell Publishing Co., Inc., $4.95 (649.1).
Brazelton demonstrates, through comparison of three mothers and their children, that "normal" children can be very different.

____. *Toddlers & Parents: A Declaration of Independence*.
Delacorte Press, Inc., 1974, $10 (649.1).
Again, Brazelton uses specific instances of behavior in toddlers, and parental reaction to that behavior to make his points. An interesting book.

*Caplan, Frank. *The First Twelve Months of Life: Your Baby's Growth Month by Month*. Grosset & Dunlap, Inc., 1973, $5.95.
An excellent resource discussing the normal development of infants.

*Fraiberg, Selma. *The Magic Years*. Charles Scribner's Sons, 1968, $7.95/$2.95 (649.1).
An encouraging, supportive book about child rearing.

Ginott, Haim G. *Between Parent and Child: New Solutions to Old Problems*. Avon Books, 1973, $1.50, Macmillan Publishing Co., 1969, $6.95 (649.1).
This highly readable book contains many specific suggestions to enhance communication between parents and their children.

Gordon, Thomas. *Parent Effectiveness Training: The Tested New Way to Raise Responsible Children*. Peter H. Wyden, Inc., 1970, $9.95, New American Library, 1975, $4.95 (649.1).
Specific suggestions for parent-child communication and interaction so that no one loses.

*Gregg, Elizabeth. *What to Do When There's Nothing to Do*. Delacorte Press, Inc., 1968, $4.95, Dell Publishing Co., 1970, 95¢ (j649.1).
This mother's handbook, prepared by the staff of the Boston Children's Medical Center, and edited by Gregg, is chockful of suggestions for entertaining your children inexpensively.

*Jones, Sandy. *Good Things for Babies*. Houghton Mifflin Co., 1976, $7.95/$4.95.
Discusses good toys, etc.

Levy, Janine Dr. *The Baby Exercise Book; The First Fifteen Months*. Random House, Inc., 1973, Pantheon Books, 1975, $7.95/$2.95.
Shows exercises that a mother and father can do with their child.

Montagu, Ashley. *Touching: The Human Significance of the Skin*. Columbia University Press, 1971, $10, Harper & Row, 1972, $1.95.
Discusses the importance of physical contact for normal development.
Newton, Niles. *The Family Book of Child Care*. Harper & Row, 1957, $9.95.
A good, comprehensive guide to child care.
Salk, Lee, and Kramer, Rita. *How to Raise a Human Being: A Parents' Guide to Emotional Health from Infancy through Adolescence*. 1969, Random House, Inc., $6.95, Warner Books, Inc., 1973, $1.50 (649.1).
Just as the title suggests, Salk and Kramer deal with the emotional health of children.
*Shiller, Jack G., M.D. *Childhood Illness—A Common Sense Approach*. Stein and Day, 1972, $7.95, 1974, $1.95.
This highly practical book will help you determine when your child's symptoms of illness are serious and when they are not, which symptoms can be treated at home, and which need medical attention. Has an excellent appendix: "Useful Over-the-Counter Drugs and Doses."
Spock, Benjamin. *Baby and Child Care*. Revised Edition, Pocket Books, Inc., $1.50, Hawthorn Books, Inc., $6.95.
This classic book on child care treats everything from development through behavior problems and illnesses.

Exercise in General

Bach, Lydia. *Awake! Aware! Alive!:* Exercises for a Vital Body. Random House, 1973, $6.95 (q613.71).
A beautifully photographed gem of an exercise book based upon Lotte Berk's philosophy of exercise. Good discussion of major body parts and how exercise affects them.
*Cooper, Kenneth, M.D. *Aerobics*. M. Evans and Co., 1968, $5.95, Bantam, 1972, $1.50 (613.71).
The classic book on aerobic fitness. Excellent discussion of aerobic exercise and its benefits.
———. *New Aerobics*. M. Evans, 1970, $5.95, Bantam, 1970, $1.50 (613.71).
Cooper's sequel to *Aerobics*. I recommend using this as an addendum to his first book.
Cooper, Mildred, and Cooper, Kenneth. *Aerobics for Women*. M. Evans, 1972, $5.95, Bantam, 1973, $1.50 (613.71).
The Cooper concept of aerobics applied to women. Short section on aerobics during pregnancy.
Henderson, Joe. *Run Gently, Run Long*. World Publications, 1974, paper $2.50
Henderson's noncompetitive approach to running is a refreshing deviation from our culture's frequently cutthroat approach to sports and physical movement. A mediative, quiet book full of good information.
*Leonard, George. *The Ultimate Athlete: Revisioning Sports, Physical Education, and the Body*. Viking Press, 1975, $10.00, Avon, 1975, $1.95 (613.7).
It is Leonard's belief that one can attain a sense of unity within oneself, indeed within the universe, through physical movement. He puts the human body back firmly where it belongs—as an equal partner to the spirit and intellect. A beautiful, thought-provoking, uplifting book. One that *everyone* should read.

*Lettvin, Maggie. *The Beautiful Machine*. Alfred A. Knopf, 1972, $10.00, Ballantine Press, 1975, $2.95 (613.71).

Lettvin has accomplished what few authors have managed to do—she has written about exercise with a sound sense of humor, as well as with great authority. She has also created a unique way of individualizing her recommended programs. Unfortunately, this is hard to find in libraries because the hardback edition consists of cards in a cardboard box—a great way to look at exercises, but one librarians frown upon. It's worth purchasing.

*Morehouse, Laurence E., and Gross, Leonard. *Total Fitness in 30 Minutes a Week*. Simon & Schuster, 1975, $7.95, and in paper, $1.95 (613.7).

I think that this unfortunate title, which, to me, smacks of sensationalism, may prevent many people from discovering the great wealth of information in this excellent book. It contains the best, most concise discussion of pulse-rated exercise that I have yet found.

Prudden, Bonnie. *How to Keep Slender and Fit After Thirty*. B. Geis Associates, 1969, $6.95, Pocket Books, Inc., $1.75 (613.71).

A good general guide to exercise, with excellent suggestions for using specific body parts. Ms. Prudden is a recognized authority in the field, and has written many other fine books as well.

Ullyot, Joan, M.D. *Women's Running*. World Publications, 1976, $2.50.

A reassuring, sensitive book written by a woman exercise physiologist and marathon runner. She deals extremely well with many of the problems and concerns of women runners—whether beginning or practiced—and offers a myriad of practical suggestions. A must for women who want to jog.

Appendix A

WEIGHT BAGS*

Materials Needed:
Heavy weight fabric (such as vinyl or canvas); different colors for each set of bags.

> 1 lb. weight— 7'' x 10''
> 2 lb. weight—10'' x 12''
> 5 lb. weight—10'' x 13''

Ribbon:Four pieces of one-inch-wide ribbon, each piece about 10 inches long.
Shot or sand: as many pounds as you need to make two weight bags. (For example, if you plan to make a set of 5-pound bags, you'll need 10 pounds of shot or sand.) Shot is easier to work with, and can be purchased in many sporting good stores.

Directions

1. Place fabric right side up.
Pin two ribbons, as shown.

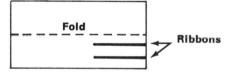

2. Fold the fabric lengthwise.
Stitch two sides, as shown.
Turn inside out.

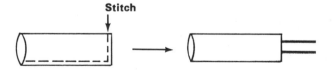

3. Fill with ½ of shot or sand for one bag.
Pin closed.
Stitch as shown.

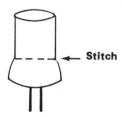

*Inspired by Bonnie Prudden's design for weight bags.

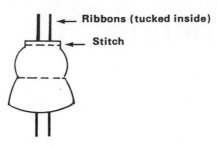

4.   Fill with the rest of the shot or sand.
Pin ribbons in as shown.
Stitch as shown.

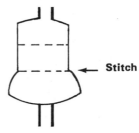

5.   Turn the bag upside down.
Stitch as shown.

6.   When you want to hold the bags in your hands, tie the ribbons in bows at each end so that they don't get in your way. When you want to use the bags on your ankles/feet/wrists, etc., tie them on, using the ribbons.

Appendix B

Body Part	# of Exercise	Name of Exercise	Stretches	Strengthens	Page #
Neck	1	Neck Rolls	x	x	27
	8	Hamstring Stretch (intensified)	x		37
	9	Inner Thigh Stretch	x		38
	11	Roll-Ups		x	40
	24	Roll Backs		x	69
	30	Angry Cat	x		85
	31	Back Tuck and Arch	x		86
Shoulders	2	Arm Circles	x	x	29
	13	Wall Push-Ups		x	43
	18	Arm Swings	x	x	59
	19	Shoulder Shrugs	x	x	60
	20	Thumbs Down		x	61
	21	Modified Push-Ups		x	62
	22	Forearm Rests		x	64
	30	Angry Cat	x		85
	40	Hip Roll	x		101
Upper Arms	2	Arm Circles	x	x	29
	13	Wall Push-Ups		x	43
	18	Arm Swings	x	x	59
	20	Thumbs Down	x	x	61
	21	Modified Push-Ups		x	62
	22	Forearm Rests		x	64
	28	Leg Overs	x	x	75
	40	Hip Roll	x		101
	48	Arm Slides	x	x	109
Lateral Abdominals	3	Hip Joint Warm-Ups	x		30
	6	Allover Stretch	x	x	34
	7	Lateral Bends	x	x	36
	23	Elbow-Knee Roll-Up	x	x	68
	26	Waist Twists	x	x	73
	27	Side Torso Raises		x	74
	28	Leg Overs	x	x	75
	29	Straddle Stretch	x	x	77
	32	Wall Walk	x	x	88
	37	Side Leg Lifts		x	98
	39	Inner Thigh Lifts		x	100
	40	Hip Roll	x	x	101

Body Part	# of Exercise	Name of Exercise	Stretches	Strengthens	Page #
Front					
Abdominals	3	Hip Joint Warm-Ups	x		30
	4	Knee Circles		x	32
	5	Ankle Circles		x	33
	6	Allover Stretch	x		34
	10	Pelvic Tilt		x	39
	11	Roll-Ups		x	40
	22	Forearm Rests		x	64
	23	Elbow-Knee Roll-Up		x	68
	24	Roll Backs		x	69
	25	Lowering Legs		x	71
	28	Leg Overs	x	x	75
	30	Angry Cat	x	x	85
	31	Back Tuck and Arch	x	x	86
	32	Wall Walk		x	88
	35	Leg Extensions (front)		x	94
	36	String of Beads	x	x	97
Lower Back	3	Hip Joint Warm-Ups	x		30
	6	Allover Stretch	x		34
	7	Lateral Bends	x	x	36
	8	Hamstring Stretch	x		37
	9	Inner Thigh Stretch	x		38
	10	Pelvic Tilt	x	x	39
	11	Roll-Ups	x		40
	16	Back Stretch	x		52
	23	Elbow-Knee Roll-Up	x		68
	25	Lowering Legs		x	71
	26	Waist Twists	x	x	73
	28	Leg Overs	x		75
	29	Straddle Stretch	x	x	77
	30	Angry Cat	x	x	85
	31	Back Tuck and Arch	x	x	86
	32	Wall Walk	x	x	88
	33	Iliopsoas Muscle Stretch and Strengthener	x	x	90
	34	Lower Back Stretch	x		91
	35	Leg Extensions (back)		x	94
	36	String of Beads	x	x	97
	40	Hip Roll	x		101
	42	Squat Stretch	x		104
Upper Back	2	Arm Circles		x	29
	6	Allover Stretch	x		34
	8	Hamstring Stretch	x		37
	9	Inner Thigh Stretch	x		38
	13	Wall Push-Ups		x	43
	18	Arm Swings	x	x	59
	20	Thumbs Down	x	x	61
	21	Modified Push-Ups		x	62

Body Part	# of Exercise	Name of Exercise	Stretches	Strengthens	Page #
	23	Elbow-Knee Roll-Up	x		68
	24	Roll Backs	x		69
	29	Straddle Stretch	x		77
	30	Angry Cat	x	x	85
	31	Back Tuck and Arch		x	86
	32	Wall Walk	x	x	88
	36	String of Beads	x		97
	42	Squat Stretch	x		104
	47	Pectoral Muscle Strengthener and Stretcher	x	x	108
	48	Arm Slides		x	109
	54	Slumping Forward	x		119
Chest	2	Arm Circles	x		29
	13	Wall Push-Ups		x	43
	18	Arm Swings	x		59
	19	Shoulder Shrugs	x		60
	20	Thumbs Down	x	x	61
	21	Modified Push-Ups		x	62
	22	Forearm Rests		x	64
	26	Waist Twists	x		73
	32	Wall Walk	x		88
	40	Hip Roll	x		101
	47	Pectoral Muscle Strengthener and Stretcher	x	x	108
	48	Arm Slides	x		109
Buttocks	7	Lateral Bends		x	36
	6	Allover Stretch	x		34
	8	Hamstring Stretch	x		37
	10	Pelvic Tilt		x	39
	14	The Doggy		x	44
	22	Forearm Rests		x	64
	25	Lowering Legs		x	71
	26	Waist Twists		x	73
	28	Leg Overs	x		75
	30	Angry Cat	x	x	85
	31	Back Tuck and Arch	x	x	86
	32	Wall Walk	x	x	88
	34	Lower Back Stretch	x		91
	35	Leg Extensions (back)		x	94
	36	String of Beads		x	97
	38	Partial Side Leg Lifts		x	99
	41	Kneeling Walk	x		103
	42	Squat Stretch	x		104
Thighs *Front*	3	Hip Joint Warm-Ups		x	30
	4	Knee Circles		x	32
	5	Ankle Circles		x	33
	6	Allover Stretch	x		34

Body Part	# of Exercise	Name of Exercise	Stretches	Strengthens	Page #
	22	Forearm Rests		x	64
	25	Lowering Legs		x	71
	32	Wall Walk		x	88
	35	Leg Extensions (front)		x	94
	41	Kneeling Walk (feet straight)		x	103
	42	Squat Stretch		x	104
	44	Knee Lifts		x	107
Side	14	The Doggy		x	44
	26	Waist Twists	x	x	73
	27	Side Torso Raises		x	74
	28	Leg Overs	x		75
	35	Leg Extensions (side)		x	94
	37	Side Leg Lifts		x	98
	38	Partial Side Leg Lifts		x	99
	39	Inner Thigh Lifts	x	x	100
	41	Kneeling Walk (toes out)		x	103
	44	Knee Lifts		x	107
Inner	3	Hip Joint Warm-Ups	x		30
	6	Allover Stretch	x		34
	9	Inner Thigh Stretch	x		38
	28	Leg Overs	x	x	75
	29	Straddle Stretch	x		77
	33	Iliopsoas Muscle Stretch	x		90
	37	Side Leg Lifts	x		98
	38	Partial Side Leg Lifts	x		99
	39	Inner Thigh Lifts		x	100
	41	Kneeling Walk (pigeon-toed)		x	103
	42	Squat Stretch	x		104
	44	Knee Lifts		x	107
Back	6	Allover Stretch	x		34
	8	Hamstring Stretch	x		37
	9	Inner Thigh Stretch	x		38
	10	Pelvic Tilt		x	39
	14	The Doggy		x	44
	22	Forearm Rests		x	64
	26	Waist Twists		x	73
	29	Straddle Stretch	x		77
	30	Angry Cat		x	85
	31	Back Tuck and Arch		x	86
	35	Leg Extensions (back)		x	94
	36	String of Beads		x	97
	38	Partial Side Leg Lifts		x	99
	42	Squat Stretch	x		104

Appendix C

EXERCISE MAT

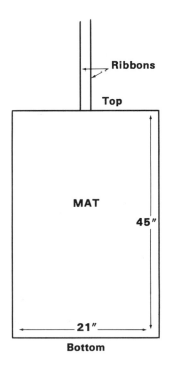

*Y*ou may or may not feel the need to have an exercise mat. If you are exercising on a grassy lawn, or at home on a carpeted floor, you probably don't need one. But if you plan to exercise on a hard floor, or on the patio, then you will need *something* to protect your spine and joints from bruising. That something can be a carpet remnant, your bath mat, or a thickly woven blanket folded several times. *Or* it can be a real, honest-to-goodness exercise mat.

It is possible to create a truly glorious exercise mat. If that interests you, use the following instructions as a guide. Then embroider, appliqué, or macrame something really wonderful into your mat.

Frankly, *I* have very little patience with sewing, and so these instructions are super simple. In fact, my nine-year-old son has created a fine little business by making mats for women in my class. If he can do it, *we* certainly can. Right?

The general idea here is to make a large "pillowcase," with two ribbons sewn into the seam that would be the bottom of the pillowcase if you held the open end up.

Here's a picture of what your exercise mat should look like when it is finished. Now for more specific instructions.

Materials needed:
1½ yards of washable, patterned, 45-inch fabric. (Dark or intricate patterns work best because they don't show the dirt.)
Two ribbons, about ¼ inch wide and 19 inches long.
Thread
One piece of polyurethane foam: 21 inches by 45 inches by 1 inch.*

Procedures
1.   Place fabric right side up on the floor.
2.   Place top of the ribbons 11 inches from the right selvage, with ribbon ends touching top of fabric. Stretch the ribbons out full length, going *down* toward the bottom of the fabric from the top of the fabric. Pin both ends in place.
3.   Fold fabric in half, lengthwise.
4.   Now, using about 10 stitches to the inch, stitch the top seam closed. Be certain that you catch the ribbons in that seam. Then stitch back and forth over the ribbons several times to make them secure.
5.   Stitch side seam closed, using same stitch length.
6.   Do *not* stitch bottom seam closed.
7.   Turn "pillowcase" right side out. The ribbons should dangle from the bottom end of the "pillowcase."
8.   Insert the foam. Fold material ends at the bottom of the "pillowcase" in.
9.   Hand stitch the bottom of the "pillowcase" closed.
10.   You're done! Unless you want to exercise right now, roll your mat up, starting at the nonribboned end. Then, wrap one ribbon around the mat, tie it to the other ribbon, and stick your mat in the closet until you're ready to use it. (The reason that I love the ribbon idea is that a flat exercise mat refuses to roll up and stay that way, and so never fits *anywhere* well.)

*Polyurethane foam comes in many densities, and under many brand names. Generally, the denser a piece of foam is, the more expensive it is, and the more protection it will provide. You can use your own good judgment in selecting a piece of foam. But if you are ever in doubt as to whether a certain piece of foam will work for you, give it the spinal test. Put it down on a hard floor, lie on it on your back, assume the Modified Roll-Up position, and pay attention to your spine. If you don't feel any pressure on your backbone from the floor, that foam is probably all right for you.

However, my friendly local expert suggests using one of the following types of foam for exercise mats:

    3- to 3½-pound 2090 polyurethane foam or
    3- to 3½-pound HR32 cirrus foam

If you shop around and are unable to find the type of foam in the size you want, you can write to my local expert for information:

THE HOUSE OF FOAM
150 Hamilton Street
Palo Alto, California 94301

These are good people, and will answer your questions honestly and well. They will also fill orders by mail, with postage and handling charges added to the price of the foam. For prices, mail them your questions, provide any pertinent information that you feel they will need to help you, and enclose a self-addressed stamped envelope.

Bibliography

The Physiology of Pregnancy and Applied Physiology

Bailey, Rosemary E. *Obstetrical and Gynecological Nursing*. Williams & Wilkins Co., 1970.

Basmajian, J. V. *Muscles Alive: Their Function Revealed by Electromyography*. 3rd Edition, Williams & Wilkins Co., 1974.

———. *Primary Anatomy*. 6th Edition, Williams & Wilkins Co., 1970.

Bieniarz, J., et al. "Aortocaval Compression by the Uterus in Late Human Pregnancy." *American Journal of Obstetrics and Gynecology* 103: 19–31, January 1, 1969.

Bookmiller, Mae M., and Bowe, George Loveridge. *Textbook of Obstetrics and Obstetrical Nursing*. W. B. Saunders Company, 1961.

Clayton, Stanley G., et al. *Obstetrics*. 12th Edition, Williams & Wilkins Co., 1972.

Eartman, N. H., and Hellman, L. M. *Williams Obstetrics*. 14th Edition, Appleton-Century-Crofts, Inc., 1971.

Fast, Julius. *You and Your Feet*. St. Martins, 1971.

Feldenkrais, Moshe. *Awareness through Movement: Health Exercises for Personal Growth*. Harper & Row, 1972.

Francis, Carl C. *Introduction to Human Anatomy*. 6th Edition, C. V. Mosby Co., 1973.

———. *The Human Pelvis*. C. V. Mosby Co., 1952.

Friesner, Arlyne, and Raff, Beverly. *Obstetric Nursing*. Medical Examination Publishing Co., 1974.

Garry, Matthew M. *Obstetrics Illustrated*. 2nd Edition, Revised 3rd Edition, Longman, Inc., 1974.

Hawkins, D. F. *Obstetrics Therapeutics*. Williams & Wilkins Co., 1974.

Howard, F. H. "Delivery in the Physiologic Position." *American Journal of Obstetrics and Gynecology* 11: 318–22, 1958.

Jacob, Stanley W., and Francone, Clarice Ashworth. *Structure and Function in Man*. W. B. Saunders Co., 1970.

Kelly, J. "Effect of Fear upon Uterine Motility." *American Journal of Obstetrics and Gynecology* 83: 576–81, 1962.

Knuttgen, Howard G., and Emerson, Kendall, Jr. "Physiological Response to Pregnancy at Rest and During Exercise." *Journal of Applied Physiology*, volume 35, May 1974.

Kraus, Hans. *Backache, Stress, and Tension*. Simon & Schuster, 1969.

———. *Clinical Treatment of Back & Neck Pain*. McGraw-Hill Book Co., 1970.

Lagerwerff, Ellen B., and Perlroth, Karen A. *Mesendieck: Your Posture and Your Pain*. Doubleday & Co., Inc., 1973.

Michele, Arthur Albert. *Orthotherapy*. M. Evans & Co., 1971.

———. *Iliopsoas: Development of Abnormalities in Man*. Charles C. Thomas, Publishers, 1962.

Naroll, F. et al. "Position of Women in Childbirth" *American Journal of Obstetrics and Gynecology* 82: 943–54, 1961.

Pike, R., and Smiciklas, H. "A Reappraisal of Sodium Restriction During Pregnancy." *International Journal of Gynecology and Obstetrics* 10: 1–8, January 1972.

Ueland, K., and Hansen, J. "Maternal Cardiovascular Dynamics: Influence of Gestational Age on Response to Postural Exercise." *American Journal of Obstetrics and Gynecology* 104: 856–64, July 15, 1969.

———. "Maternal Cardiovascular Dynamics: Posture and Uterine Contractions." *American Journal of Obstetrics and Gynecology* 103: 1–7, January 1, 1969.

Willson, J. Robert. *Obstetrics and Gynecology*. 5th Edition, C. V. Mosby Co., 1975.

Kinesiology

Cooper, John M., and Glassow, Ruth B. *Kinesiology*. Revised 3rd Edition, C. V. Mosby Co., 1972.

Kelley, David L. *Kinesiology: Fundamentals of Motion Description*. Prentice-Hall, 1971.

Rasch, Philip J., and Burke, Roger K. *Kinesiology & Applied Anatomy: The Science of Human Movement*. Lea & Febiger, 1974.

Steindler, Arthur. *Kinesiology: Of the Human Body under Normal and Pathological Conditions*. Charles C. Thomas, 1973.

Wells, Katherine F. *Kinesiology: The Scientific Basis of Human Motion*. W. B. Saunders Co., 1971.

Physiology of Exercise and Exercise in General

Cooper, Kenneth. *Aerobics*. M. Evans & Co., 1968.

———. *New Aerobics*. M. Evans & Co., 1970.

———, and Cooper, Mildred. *Aerobics for Women*. M. Evans & Co., 1972.

Etter, Mildred F. *Exercises for the Prone Patient*. Wayne State University Press, 1968.

Johnson, Harry J. *Creative Walking for Physical Fitness*. Grosset & Dunlap, Inc., 1970.

Jokl, E. and McClellan, J. T., eds. *Exercise and Cardiac Death*. University Park Press, 1971.

Kasch, Fred W., and Boyer, John L. *Adult Fitness: Principles and Practices*. All American Productions and Publications, 1968.

Konishi, Frank. *Exercise Equivalents of Foods: A Practical Guide for the Overweight*. Southern Illinois University Press, 1975.

MacKay, Richard T. *Exercise, Rest, and Relaxation*. William C. Brown Co., Publishers, 1970.

Morehouse, Laurence E., and Gross, Leonard. *Total Fitness in 30 Minutes a Week*. Simon & Schuster, 1975.

———, and Miller, Augustus T., Jr. *Physiology of Exercise*. 6th Edition, C. V. Mosby Co., 1971.

Morse, Robert L., et al. *Exercise and the Heart: Guidelines for Exercise Programs*. Charles C. Thomas, publishers, 1974.

Naughton, John, and Hellerstein, Herman K., eds. *Exercise Testing and Exercise Training in Coronary Heart Disease*. Academy Press, 1973.

Steincroft, Peter Joseph. *You Live as You Breathe*. David McKay Co., Inc., 1967.

Books Containing Exercises Specifically for Maintaining Fitness During Pregnancy

Bach, Lydia. *Awake! Awake! Alive!* Random House, 1973.

Bing, Elisabeth. *Moving Through Pregnancy*. Bobbs-Merrill Co., Inc., 1975.

Davis, M. Edward, and Maisel, Edward. *Have Your Baby, Keep Your Figure*. Simon & Schuster, n d

Kounovsky, Nicholas Alexis. *The Joy of Feeling Fit*. E. P. Dutton & Co., 1971.

Lettvin, Maggie. *The Beautiful Machine*. Alfred A. Knopf, 1972.

Prudden, Bonnie. *How to Keep Slender and Fit after Thirty*. B. Geis Associates, 1969.

Index